Programmer's Phrasebook

Ian A. Clark

— Sigma Press —

Wilmslow, United Kingdom

First published in 1991 by
Sigma Press, 1 South Oak Lane, Wilmslow, Cheshire SK9 6AR, England.

British Library Cataloguing in Publication Data
A CIP catalogue record for this book is available from the British Library.

ISBN: 1-85058-194-0

Typesetting and design by
Sigma Hi-Tech Services Ltd

Printed in Malta by
Interprint Ltd.

Distributed by
John Wiley & Sons Ltd., Baffins Lane, Chichester, West Sussex, England.

Preface

This guide tells you how to make effective use of Zortech C* running under MS-DOS*. It can be used also with other C compilers. Besides explaining the essentials of the language in simple unambiguous terms, it will encourage you to view C in a new, creative light, even if you already have some knowledge of C, or another computer language. There are also two Appendixes containing summary information in a novel useful form not available elsewhere: a list of Standard Library Functions in the proposed new ANSI Standard (which Zortech C supports) and a comparative account of the format string of both printf() and scanf().

This guide has some remarkable features, unique to the present series. It is task-oriented, not function-oriented. Most books on computer languages (and C in particular) are function-oriented. That is, they go through the "functions" of C (whether built-in functions or language constructs) one at a time, taking each function in turn and exhaustively describing its options. This leaves you to work out in detail just what function to choose for a given task and how to apply it. Even after learning the syntax of the language you may be unsure of how to use it to perform a task you can do quite well in another language.

What you need then is a "traveller's phrasebook", not a language grammar. Something based on idioms used in their proper context, not lists of irregular verbs. This book does that. It explains exactly how to perform a whole range of standardised programming tasks, with readily adapted examples. These tasks are precise ones, not generic ones. They include most of what a PC program commonly does.

The tasks and their solutions are described, not in the special jargon of C, but in a standardised vocabulary of computing terms to ensure comparability with those you already understand. These terms are capitalised in the text and defined in Appendix A. Computer terms not capitalised are to be understood informally. Unless you realise this, you might think the use of capitals is capricious.

The standard set of tasks and their vocabulary comprise the Comparable Construct Classification System (C3S). In the PC Pocket Guide series there are companion C3S books for other popular programming languages including BASIC and Pascal. Any two C3S books share the same structure of numbered sections. Thus, in each book, 7.9.3 tells you how to loop 10 times and 9.1.5 tells you how to emit a "cuckoo" sound.

The entire set of C3S books will enable you:

❑ to become speedily fluent in a second language

❑ to transfer your programming skills rapidly between two or more languages, even if you are not using them all the time

❑ to undertake a detailed comparison of "power" between any two languages

❑ to decide whether another language can fulfil your requirements better than one you already know.

Even if you know C already and wish to learn another language, get this book as well. It improves understanding to see a programming construct expressed, not only in a language you are just learning, but also in one with which you are familiar.

Throughout the book:

❑ Zortech C refers to the Zortech Inc, C Optimising Compiler.

❑ MS-DOS refers to Microsoft MS-DOS Operating System.

❑ IBM is the registered trademark of International Business Machines Corporation.

❑ PC refers to any computer compatible with the IBM Personal Computer range.

❑ DOS refers to either MS-DOS or IBM PCDOS.

Ian A. Clark

Contents

1

Applications: Building, Running and Changing

C is a Compiled Language. A Program is written in C as a text File (or ASCII File), i.e. as a series of legible lines each terminated by Carriage Return + Linefeed Characters. Suppose its name is MYAPPL.C. It can be displayed by the DOS TYPE Command and can be written and read by using EDLIN or any other DOS text Editor. In practice, using Zortech C, MYAPPL.C would be written and maintained using Zortech's own Editor, ZED. ZED offers not only full-screen editing and advanced editing Functions but also comprises an integrated development environment for single-Program Applications, allowing the loaded Program to be Compiled, Linked and Run at any stage with a single Keystroke. The interactive ZED session resumes automatically upon Program Termination. Comparable facilities can be expected from other vendors' C Language Systems operating under DOS.

In what follows the standard tasks of C3S are performed either as Statements in the C Language, or as Commands or interactions with the ZED Editor, or as Commands to DOS. The first two kinds are distinguishable by context and form, the C Language Statements being entirely in computer-style text like this: ABC.def.(123) and containing no Keystroke Names (like {Return} or {Alt-V}).

If the Command is intended for DOS it is shown preceded by the DOS System Prompt, C>. For simplicity it is assumed that Zortech C has been correctly installed and resides in the "current" Directory on drive C: which is the "default" Drive ("current" and "default" being DOS terminology, which will not be explained here). If your DOS System happens to give a different Prompt then this is to be understood in place of C>.

1.1 Run an Application

A C Program called (say) MYAPPL.C is written by the programmer as a text File. To Run it, MYAPPL.C is first converted to a File called MYAPPL.OBJ using ZC, the vendor's two-pass C Compiler. Files having extension .OBJ contain cross-references to other .OBJ and .LIB Files plus machine code strings and are similar to "assembled" Programs, or those compiled by other Language Compilers. MYAPPL.OBJ is then "linked", i.e. combined with other pre-existing .OBJ Files, to form an

1

Executable File named MYAPPL.EXE. If MYAPPL.EXE fits the so-called "tiny model" it may then be converted into a File named MYAPPL.COM. Files of type .COM resemble DOS external Commands and have the advantage of loading faster than .EXE Files.

1.1.1 Start an interactive session
Directly from the DOS Prompt:
```
C>zed
```
or:
```
C>zed myappl.c
```

1.1.2 Run an Application whilst within an interactive session
Select Menu: Other. Select cOmpile. Enter Null for both ZC Flags and Run Parameters. This is equivalent to:
{Alt-C} {Return} ...Wait... {Return}
This compiles and links the Program MYAPPL.C currently within ZED, and Runs it under DOS.
To Run the Program again without alteration:
Select Menu: Other. Select Dos. Enter: myappl This is equivalent to:
{Alt-D} myappl {Return}

1.1.3 Run an Application directly whilst at the DOS prompt
```
C>myappl
```
The Application Program must first have been compiled and linked by the System to produce an Application File called MYAPPL.EXE. See 1.1.2.

1.2 Terminate a Running Application

Programs in some other Languages, e.g. BASIC and APL, are intimately bound up with their Language Systems. However C Programs are entirely independent of Zortech C once they have been Compiled and converted into .EXE or .COM Files. This section deals with the C3S tasks of terminating both a Program and the Language System, tasks which are closely connected in some Languages, although not in C. In what follows therefore, the "interactive session" refers to the ZED Editor, whereas the Run refers only to the Compiled Program.

1.2.1 Quit from interactive session and return to DOS
Select Menu: File. Select: eXit.
Reply: y to any verification questions.
Alternative quick keys:
{Alt-V}
saves all changes and exits.
Or:
{Alt-Q} {Alt-X}

abandons changes and exits. If no changes have been made then {Alt-Q} can be omitted.

1.2.2 Terminate the Run by means of a Program Statement
```
exit(0);
```
Terminates normally. The Run also terminates normally when Control drops through the outermost Block {...}. In a well-structured Program, `exit(0)` is rarely needed.

Or, to return a non-Zero value of ERRORLEVEL to DOS, replace (0) with the required Integer Value.

1.3 Build an Application

A C Program called (say) MYAPPL.C is written by the programmer as a text File. Novices to C who are familiar with DOS and text Files should therefore understand that any permissible operations upon a text File can in principle be used to write and maintain C Programs. However the ZED Editor has some unique and useful features, so the C3S tasks of writing the Program are described in terms of what ZED can offer.

One useful feature of ZED is that it is capable of running the Compiler, ZC, not only upon saved versions of the File being Edited, but also upon the loaded image of the File in Memory, called the "buffer". It is also capable of holding up to five File images in its five buffers at once, and transferring control and sections of text between buffers.

1.3.1 Begin a new Application called MYAPPL
Directly from the DOS Prompt:
```
C>zed myappl.c
```
Within ZED:
```
{Alt-E} myappl.c{Return}
```

1.3.2 Inspect the Program of existing Application MYAPPL
Directly from the DOS Prompt:
```
C>type myappl.c
```
Or:
```
C>zed myappl.c
```
then use {PgUp}, {PgDn} to scroll through the Program.

1.3.3 Insert a new Program Statement occupying one entire line into the Application MYAPPL
Place Cursor at end of line which the new Statement is to follow (move Cursor to line, then press {End}). Press {Return} to make an empty line. Then type the line.

1.3.4 Alter by overtyping an existing Program line
Place Cursor on the required line and overtype it.

Press {Ins} to toggle between OVERTYPE and INSERT modes.
Recompile when satisfied, using 1.1.2.

1.3.5 Insert a Comment occupying one entire line into the Application MYAPPL

Insert a line:
```
/* This is a Comment */
```

1.3.6 Append a trailing Comment to an existing Program line
```
z+=1;
```
becomes:
```
z+=1; /* This is a Comment */
```
Tab may be used in place of optional Space before /*..., or both
together.

1.3.7 Insert a Comment inside an existing Program line
A Comment can be inserted anywhere provided no Tokens (see 15.1) are
split, e.g.
```
z+=1;
```
might become:
```
z/* This is a Comment */+=1;
```
whereas this corrupts the Syntax:
```
z+/* This is a Comment */=1;
```

1.3.8 Delete an entire Program line
Place Cursor at start of line. Press {f9}.

1.3.9 Delete a sequence of Program lines
Place Cursor at start of first line to be deleted.
Press {f6} (this sets down a so-called TAG).
Move Cursor down to start of first line NOT to be deleted.
Press {f4} (this deletes lines between TAG and Cursor).
To verify whereabouts of TAG if desired at any time, press Key {f5}
twice. This will indicate the extent of the current block.

1.3.10 Move a sequence of Program lines to beneath a destination line elsewhere in the Program
Delete the sequence of lines as in 1.3.9.
Place Cursor at start of line AFTER the destination line. Press {f3}.

1.3.11 Copy a sequence of Program lines to beneath a destination line elsewhere in the Program
Delete the sequence of lines as 1.3.9.
Press {f3} to bring them back in the same place.
Place Cursor at start of line *after* the destination line. Press {f3} again.

1.3.12 Copy a sequence of Program lines into another Program

Choose an unused buffer, e.g. 2, by pressing {Alt-2}
Load the target Program into it as follows:
 {Alt-E}target.c{Return}
View buffer 1 by pressing {Alt-1}
Delete the sequence of lines as in 1.3.9.
View buffer 2 by pressing {Alt-2}
Place Cursor at start of line AFTER the destination line and press {f3}.

1.3.13 Finalise the Application MYAPPL for release to other users.

Directly from the DOS Prompt:
 C>zc myappl
Within ZED:
{Alt-C} {Return} ...Wait... {Return}
The finalised Application normally consists of a single File:
MYAPPL.EXE. Other Files involved in the process, MYAPPL.C and
MYAPPL.OBJ, are retained by the programmer.
For larger Programs, several .OBJ files can be combined by running
LINK directly.
To generate a so-called "tiny model" Application: MYAPPL.COM
instead of the usual MYAPPL.EXE, specify the Compiler flag: −mt.
Thus:
 {Alt-C} −mt{Return} ...Wait... {Return}

1.3.14 Save an updated version of the Application MYAPPL

Within ZED: {Alt-S}

1.3.15 Create a separately updatable copy of the Application MYAPPL called MYAPPL2

Directly from the DOS Prompt:
 C>copy myappl.c myappl2.c C>zc myappl2
ZC will compile and link MYAPPL2.C to produce Files MYAPPL2.OBJ
and MYAPPL2.EXE.
Within ZED:
{Alt-S} {Alt-2}
{Alt-E}myappl2.c{Return}
{Alt-I}myappl.c{Return} {Alt-S}

This saves the existing File, MYAPPL.C, changes to buffer no. 2
(assumed unused), specifies that the File being Edited is called
MYAPPL2.C, then reads in a copy of MYAPPL.C and saves it as
MYAPPL2.C

1.3.16 What if the Application name MYAPPL2 is already in use?

Directly from the DOS Prompt, the existing Files MYAPPL2.* are replaced without warning.

Within ZED, the contents of the existing MYAPPL2.C will appear in the new buffer immediately after:

...{Alt-E}myappl2.c{Return}

1.3.17 Erase the Program of the Application MYAPPL whilst within an interactive session

{Alt-D} erase myappl.c{Return}

1.3.18 Erase the Application MYAPPL entirely whilst within an interactive session

{Alt-D} erase myappl.c{Return}
{Alt-Q}

2

Compute a Numeric Value and assign it to a Variable

C supports the conventional concept of Assignment of a computed Expression to a Variable and most of the processing in a Program is specified to be carried out by Assignment. This chapter treats Numeric Assignments, whereas Chapter 3 treats String Assignments.

2.1 Variables

C supports the concept of a Named Variable. A Variable, z, must be "declared" in advance of Assigning a Value to it, which allocates Memory space to the Variable, according to the Type of Variable. However it can optionally be "initialised" with a Value in the Statement which declares it (see 2.1.1). If this is not done the Variable's Value is initially garbage.

This section describes what constitutes a valid Variable Name and shows how Variables are specified.

2.1.1 Specify the intention to use a Named Variable
```
int j;
long jj;
unsigned uj;
unsigned long ujj;
float z;
double zz;
```
or:
```
int j = 123;
```
or:
```
int i, j, k;
```
or:
```
int j[20];
```
or:
```
int j[] = {111, 22, 3, 44, 5555};
```
For global Variables only. Specifies an Array of as many Terms as there are Values in { ... }, in this case corresponding to:
```
int j[4];
```
or:
```
extern int j;
```
Declares j to be an external Integer Variable, but assumes Memory is allocated in another Program.

Similarly for long, etc. in place of int in each of the above.

2.1.2 Where should the specification be placed?
For Variables for which the scope to be confined to a given Block, declarations should be placed at the top of that Block.

For Variables which are external to all Program Bodies, place the specification after all #include... and #define..., but before the Main Program Header and any Subroutine specification which uses them.

2.1.3 Can Variables be initialised when first specified?
Yes. Note, however, any implementation restrictions of certain Compilers for Variables which are Localised in a given Program Body.

2.1.4 Do Variable Names follow the same rules as other kinds of Identifier?
Yes. See 15.1.3.

2.1.5 Does the choice of Name influence the Type of Variable?
No. Conventionally, however, Identifiers entirely in Uppercase are understood to be Named Constants specified by #define...

2.1.6 What can the first Character of a Name be?
One of the letters: (A...Z a...z)
or Underscore (_)

2.1.7 What Characters can be used in a Name?
The letters: (A...Z a...z)
The numerals: (0...9)
Underscore (_)

2.1.8 Are Uppercase and Lowercase Letters distinguished?
Yes.

2.1.9 How long can a Variable Name be?
127 Characters or less.

2.1.10 How many Characters of a Variable Name are distinguished?
Up to 127 Characters.

2.2 Change the Value of a Variable at Run-time

A Variable acts like a storage element for a Value. Consequently the Value of a Variable, z, can be changed freely during a Run by Assigning an Expression to z, even one involving its own existing Value. Note that although the Value (z+1) can be Assigned back to z in the manner common to many Languages, C also has special incrementing and decrementing constructs (see 2.2.4).

Assume the following declarations throughout this section:
```
int i, j; double x, y, z, a, b, c, temp;
```

2.2.1 Make Z become 99
```
z = 99;
```

2.2.2 Make Z become Y+3
```
z = y + 3;
```
or:
```
z = y + 3.0;
```

2.2.3 Does it matter if Y and Z are not of the same Type?
No. Conversion will take place automatically between Numeric Types. All computations are performed in double precision and then converted to less precise Types.

2.2.4 Increment Z by 1
```
z = z + 1;
```
or:

```
 z+=1;
```
or:
```
 z++;
```
or:
```
 ++z;
```
The Operator ++ can be applied to Variables embedded in Expressions. Thus if (z==2) prior to:
```
 y = z++ + 1;
```
y becomes 3, then z is incremented to 3. Likewise in:
```
 y = ++z + 1;
```
z is incremented to 3, then y becomes 4.

2.2.5 Negate Z
```
 z = -z;
```

2.2.6 Z and Y exchange Values
```
 temp = z; z = y; y = temp;
```

2.3 Various Numeric Values

This section shows how C Assigns Numeric Values to Variables of different Types, also the permitted range and style of Numeric Constant, including Boolean, Hexadecimal and Octal forms.

Assume the following declarations throughout this section:
```
 int j; unsigned uj; long jj; unsigned long ujj;
 float z; double zz;
```

2.3.1 Assign highest Value to an Integer Variable
```
 j       = 32767;
 uj = 65535;
 jj= 2147483647;
 ujj = 4294967293;
```
or:
```
 j       = 0x7FFF;
 uj = 0xFFFF;
 jj= (long) 0x7FFFFFFF;
 ujj = 0xFFFFFFFF;
```
or:
```
 #include <limits.h>
 ...
 j = INT_MAX;
 uj = UINT_MAX;
 jj = LONG_MAX;
 ujj = ULONG_MAX;
```

2.3.2 Assign lowest Value to an Integer Variable

```
j = -32768;
uj = 0;
jj = -2147483648;
ujj = 0;
```
or:
```
j = 0x8000;
jj = (long) 0x80000000;
```
or:
```
#include <limits.h>
...
j = INT_MIN;
jj = LONG_MIN;
```

2.3.3 Assign longest decimal fraction to a Non-Integer Variable

```
zz = 1.1234512345123451; /* 16 decimal places */
```

2.3.4 Assign highest Value to a Non-Integer Variable ("machine infinity")

```
z = 3.40282367E+38;
```
or:
```
zz = 1.7976931348623151E+308;
```
Assigning a higher Value causes "machine infinity" to be placed in zz. Thus:
```
z = 1E99;
```
results in: $(z == 3.40282367E+38)$
Similarly:
```
zz = 1E999;
```
results in: $(zz == 1.7976931348623151E+308)$

2.3.5 Assign lowest Positive Value to a Non-Integer Variable

```
z = 5.8774722E-39
```
Assigning a lower Value causes Zero to be placed in z.
```
zz = 1.1125369292536018E-308;
```
Assigning a lower Value causes Zero to be placed in zz.

2.3.6 Assign 9.9 to a Non-Integer Variable

```
zz = 9.9;
```

2.3.7 Assign 10 to the power of 30 to a Non-Integer Variable

```
zz = 1E30;
```

2.3.8 Assign Zero to a Variable

```
zz = 0;
jj = 0L; /* Constant of Type: (long) */
```

2.3.9 Assign True to a Variable
```
j = 1;
```
or:
```
#define TRUE 1
...
j = TRUE;
```

2.3.10 Assign False to a Variable
```
j = 0;
```
or:
```
#define FALSE 0
...
j = FALSE;
```

2.3.11 Assign Hexadecimal FF to a Variable
```
j = 0xFF;
```
or:
```
j = 0xff;
```
or:
```
j = 0x00ff;
```
or:
```
j = '\xFF';
```

2.3.12 Assign Octal 377 to a Variable
```
j = 0377; /* preceding Zero Digit specifies Octal */
j = '\377';
```

2.4 Named Constants

C supports the concept of a Named Constant, i.e. a Constant which is given an Identifier like a Variable so that it can be altered in the Program by changing one easily located Statement. Specifying a Named Constant in C is a special case of specifying, to the pre-processor, that a given string of Characters (the Name) must be replaced throughout with another string of Characters (a Numeral), which is the role of the #define Statement.

2.4.1 Specify the intention to use a Named Constant
```
#define MAX_ITERATIONS 10
```
or:
```
#define PI 3.141592653589794
```
or:
```
const int max_iterations = 10;
```

2.4.2 Change the Value of a Constant prior to Running
Overtype the Assignment Statement which initialises the Constant, then recompile.

2.5 Simple Arithmetic Operators

Arithmetic Operators in C follow the conventional usage of Plus (+),
Hyphen (-) for minus and negation, Asterisk (*) for multiplication
and Slash (/) for Division. Percent (%) is used for the Remainder,
i%j, of dividing Integer i by Integer j. Unlike other Languages,
arithmetic Operators are not provided for exponentiation, etc., for which
the standard library Function pow() should be used.

Throughout this section, x and y will be used, but these may be replaced
by any type of Numeric Variable, Constant or Expression in Parentheses.

2.5.1 Are the same Operators used for all Types of Number?
Yes, except that % can be used between Integers only.

2.5.2 X Plus Y
```
x+y
```

2.5.3 X Minus Y
```
x-y
```

2.5.4 X Multiplied by Y
```
x*y
```

2.5.5 X Divided by Y
```
x/y
```

2.5.6 Negation of X
```
-x
```

2.5.7 Square of X
```
x*x
```

2.5.8 Square Root of X
Not supported in C. Use 2.7.14.

2.5.9 X to Power of Y
Not supported in C. Use:
```
#include <math.h>
...
z = pow(x,y);
```
y can be Zero, Negative, Integer or Non-Integer.

2.5.10 Reciprocal of X
```
1/x
```

2.5.11 The Quotient of I by J (Integer Division)
```
i/j
```

assuming `i` and `j` are Integers. More generally:
```
((int) i)/((int) j)
```

2.5.12 The Remainder of I by J (I Modulo J)
```
i%j
```

2.6 Several Operations in a single Expression

Arithmetic Operators follow conventional precedence rules when several are used in an Expression without Parentheses. However nested Parentheses (...(...)...) can be used conventionally to force them to be applied in any desired order. Sample constructs are given below.

2.6.1 W times (U plus V)
```
w*(u+v)
```

2.6.2 (U plus V) times W
```
(u+v)*w
```

2.6.3 (U times V) plus W
```
(u*v)+w
```
or:
```
u*v+w
```

2.6.4 W plus (U times V)
```
w+(u*v)
```
or:
```
w+u*v
```

2.6.5 (U plus V) divided by W
```
(u+v)/w
```

2.6.6 (U plus V) divided by (Y plus Z)
```
(u+v)/(y+z)
```

2.6.7 Roots of Quadratic Equation with coefficients A,B,C
```
double z1, z2, a, b, c;
...
z1 = (-b + sqrt(b*b - 4*a*c))/(2*a);
z2 = (-b - sqrt(b*b - 4*a*c))/(2*a);
```

2.6.8 In what order are Operators performed?
In the following order of precedence (Tokens inside [...] have equal precedence):
Innermost parentheses first: () []
[-> .]
[! ~ ++ -- + - * & sizeof] --all used as unary Operators,

```
[ * / % ]
[ + - ] [ << >> ] [ < <= > >= ] [ == != ]
& ^ | && || ? :
[ = += -= *= /= %= &= ^= |= <<= >>= ] ,
```
Left to right.

2.7 Common Numeric Functions

C offers all of the common Numeric Functions, but as library Functions
resembling user-written Functions, not as primitives built into the
Language itself. This removes the pressure on the design of the
Functions themselves not to overload the Language with rarely-used
primitives and reserved words, but has allowed Functions to proliferate,
plus a tendency for different vendors to supply what they think fit. Use
this section to look up the Zortech C constructs for the usual (C3S)
mathematical functions. For a full list of Functions in the ANSI standard
"math" library see Appendix C.

Throughout this section assume the following line to precede in the
Program:
```
#include <math.h>
```

2.7.1 Make Z the Value of Pi
```
z = 3.141592653589794;
```
or:
```
z = acos(-1.0);
```

2.7.2 sin X
```
sin(x)
```

2.7.3 cos X
```
cos(x)
```

2.7.4 tan X
```
tan(x)
```

2.7.5 arctan Y
```
atan(y)
```
or:
```
atan2(y,x)
```
the "four quadrant" arctan of y/x, y and x both doubles, each either
Positive or Negative.

2.7.6 arcsin Y
```
asin(y)
```

14

2.7.7 arccos Y
```
acos(y)
```

2.7.8 Hyperbolic Functions
```
sinh(x)
cosh(x)
tanh(x)
```

2.7.9 Exponential Function of X
```
exp(x)
```

2.7.10 Natural Logarithm of X (to the base e)
```
log(x)
```

2.7.11 Logarithm of X to the base 10
```
log10(x)
```

2.7.12 Logarithm of X to the base 2
```
#define log2(x) (log(x)/log(2))
```

2.7.13 The whole-number part of X only
```
z = floor(x);
```
WARNING: `(x== -3.8)` gives `(z== -4.0)`.
Or:
```
(void) modf(x,&z);
```
performs correctly for x<0: `(x== -3.8)` gives `(z== -3.0)`.

2.7.14 The nearest whole-number to X
```
z = floor(x+.5); /*assumes x is positive*/
```
or:
```
z = sgn(x) * floor(fabs(x) + 0.5);
```
`sgn(x)` is as defined in 2.7.13.

2.7.15 The fractional part of X
```
double ix; /* to hold discarded Integer part */
...
z = modf(x,&ix);
```

2.7.16 The absolute Value of X
```
fabs(x);
```

2.7.17 The signum of X (-1, 0, 1)
```
#define sgn(x) ((x>0)?1 : (x==0)?0 : -1)
...
z = sgn(x);
```

2.7.18 The square-root of X
```
sqrt(x);
```

2.7.19 Make Z the larger of X and Y
```
z = max(x,y);
```

2.7.20 Make Z the smaller of X and Y
```
z = min(x,y);
```

2.7.21 Print the Binary representation of X
```
printbinary(x);
...
printbinary( int x )
{
int i;
for (i=0; i<16; i++, x<<=1)
putchar('0'+(x<0));
}
```

2.7.22 Print the Octal representation of X
```
printf("%o",x);
```

2.7.23 Print the Hexadecimal representation of X
```
printf("%X",x);
```

2.7.24 Make Z a random Integer between 1 and 6 (dice)
```
z = 1 + (int) ((rand() * 6.0) / 32768.0);
```

2.7.25 Make Z a random Non-Integer between 0 and 1
```
z = rand() / 32768.0;
```

2.7.26 Toss a coin, printing HEADS or TAILS
```
char *coin[] = {"HEADS", "TAILS"};
...
puts( coin[ rand() < 16384 ] );
```

2.7.27 Toss a biased coin (probability of HEADS is P)
```
char *coin[] = {"HEADS", "TAILS"};
double p;
...
puts( coin[ rand() < (p*32768.0) ] );
```

2.7.28 Set starting seed for random generation from the Clock
```
#include <time.h>
...
srand( clock() % 32768 );
```

16

2.8 Construct Array of Terms all the same Type

C supports the concept of Array, of 1-D, 2-D or higher dimension. An Array can have any Type of Term, but Terms must be all of the same Type (but see Structures, 2.9).

The concept is supported in a way unique to C, however, which generalises the notion of incrementing a Pointer by adding an Integer to it. Thus p+3 does not increment Pointer p by 3 Bytes but 3w Bytes, where w is the size of the target Type of p in Bytes. The construct p[3] means the same as *(p+3) to the Compiler. It follows that either Pointer Syntax *(a+i) or Array syntax a[i] may be used no matter if a is declared int *a; or int a[N].

In the latter case, N Terms of Type (int) are reserved and the simple Expression a returns a Pointer Value to the first Term, just as does &(a[0]). In the former case however no space is reserved and the Pointer Value a is initially garbage.

2.8.1 Can Arrays be nested?
No.

2.8.2 Specify an Array A of N Terms
 int a[N];
int can be replaced by any desired Type specifier.

2.8.3 Can N be Zero?
Yes.

2.8.4 Can N be Negative?
No.

2.8.5 Can N be Non-Integer?
No.

2.8.6 Specify a two dimensional Array A of 3 by 5 Terms
 int a[3][5];

2.8.7 Can an Array have higher dimension than 2?
Yes, e.g. int a[3][5][7];

2.8.8 Specify the minimum Index of an Array A
Not supported in C. Arrays must start at [0].

2.8.9 Find the size of an existing Array A
 int a[N], z;
 ...
 z = sizeof a;
 printf("Size of a is %d",z);

2.8.10 Is there any range checking?
No.

2.8.11 Place 99 in 1-dimensional Array A as the Term having Index 2
```
int a[N];
...
a[2] = 99;
```

2.8.12 Place 99 in 2-dimensional Array A as the Term having Indexes I and J
```
int a[20][20];
...
a[i][j] = 99;
```

2.8.13 Index an Array A with SUNDAY, MONDAY, I
```
enum day {SUNDAY, MONDAY, TUESDAY, WEDNESDAY,
          THURSDAY, FRIDAY, SATURDAY};
int a[7];
...
printf("%d %d", a[SUNDAY], a[MONDAY]);
```

2.8.14 Add two Arrays A and B Term-by-Term
```
int j, a[N], b[N], result[N];
...
for (j=0; j<N; j++) result[j] = a[j] + b[j];
```

2.8.15 Sum all Terms in an Array A
```
int j, a[N], z;
...
z = 0;
for (j=0; j<N; j++) z += a[j];
```

2.8.16 Construct Array A having Terms: 0,1,2,3,...
```
int j, a[N];
...
for (j=0; j<N; j++) a[j] = j;
```

2.8.17 Count the Terms in an Array A
```
int a[N], z;
...
z = sizeof a)/(sizeof a[0]);
```

2.8.18 Find the maximum Term in an Array A
```
int j, a[N], z;
...
for (j=1, z=a[0]; j<(sizeof a); j++) z=max(z,a[j]);
```

2.8.19 Find the minimum Term in an Array A

```
int j, a[N], z;
...
for (j=1, z=a[0]; j<(sizeof a); j++) z =
   min(z,a[j]);
```

2.8.20 Release the Memory allocated to Arrays A and B

Localise the Arrays a[] and b[] within a given Block {...}. Then Memory used by a[] and b[] will be released on exit from the Block.

2.9 Construct a Structure having Terms of different Types

C supports the concept of a Structure, a Type of data item consisting of a list of Terms of possibly different Types. Any Type can be used as a Term, including Structures and Arrays of Structures (but not variable length lists). This gives you an unlimited capability to specify new, complex data Types (see 2.9.3).

The Value of such a Structure is held as a contiguous sequence of Bytes in Memory (so that sizeof will work). Normally padding Bytes are interspersed so that Integers, etc. do not straddle word (double-Byte) boundaries. This speeds up Assignments to individual Terms on 16 and 32 Bit processors. However this feature (called "alignment") can be turned off by the −a Compiler flag.

2.9.1 What Types are permissible in a Structure?

All Types, including user-specified ones.

2.9.2 Can Structures be nested?

Yes.

2.9.3 Specify the intention to use a named Structure, FAM

```
struct {...} fam;
```
or:
```
struct family {...};
struct family fam;
```

This specifies a Variable fam to be of the Type: struct family which is previously specified. The (optional) Identifier: family is called the "structure tag". This technique enables several Variables to be specified having the same (Named) Structure.

2.9.4 Place forenames, ages, heights of three children into the Structure FAM together with their surname

```
struct childrecord {
  char *forename;
  int age;
```

```
  float height;
  };
struct {
char *surname;
struct childrecord child[3];
} fam = { "Jacobson",
  "Reuben", 21, 2.01,
  "Joseph", 12, 1.89,
  "Benjamin", 8, 0.91,
  };
```

2.9.5 Make Z the Value of a particular Term within Structure FAM

```
z = fam.child[2].age;
```

2.9.6 Make F a copy of the entire Structure FAM

```
struct family fam, f; ...; f = fam;
```

Structure Assignments are introduced in the draft ANSI standard and are supported by Zortech C.

2.9.7 Make a particular Term within FAM take the Value Z

```
fam.child[2].age = z;
```

3

Compute a String Value and assign it to a Variable

There is no distinct String Type in C. Instead Arrays of Type (char) are used and handled using Pointer Syntax rather than Array Syntax (see 2.8).

Note the following significant inconsistency in the treatment of (char) between Arrays and non-Array Values, viz. char c; declares c to be of Type (char) which is equivalent here to (int), a 2 Byte, not a 1 Byte Value. The Assignment:

```
c = 'A';
```

places `'A'` (ASCII 65) into the low Byte of c and sets the high Byte to Null, whereas:

```
c = 'AB';
```

places `'A'` in the high Byte and `'B'` in the low Byte of c. However declaring s either as:

```
char *s;
```

or:

```
char s[N];
```

causes s to be treated as (the Pointer to) an Array of 1-Byte Terms, each capable of holding an ASCII Character Value.

There are no String primitives in the Language apart from the construct `"HALLO"` (a Literal Constant actually 6 Bytes long including the final Null). All String processing is performed using Functions contained in the standard library "string" (see Appendix C for the ANSI version). Strings in C are conventionally handled as ASCIIZ Strings, that is, sequences of ASCII Values in successive Bytes terminating with a Null Byte. For all purposes the first Null Byte encountered defines the length of the String. Therefore:

```
char s[5] = "HALLO";
```

defines s to be a 6 Byte ASCIIZ String, the 6th Byte being Null. The definition:

```
char s[4] = "HALLO";
```

is dangerous. ANSI specifies that this should actually place `'H'` `'A'` `'L'` `'L'` `'O'` in s[0] ... s[4] but not set the next Byte after s[4] to Null. However s will almost certainly misbehave when treated as a String by the "string" standard Functions, which are likely to overshoot the end.

All the "string" library Functions begin with: `str...` Throughout this section assume that all calls to `str...` Functions are preceded in the Program by the line:

```
#include <string.h>
```

3.1 Various String Constants

A Literal Constant can be specified enclosed either in Quotes or Apostrophes, but the two are not equivalent. `"AB"` specifies a 3 Byte ASCIIZ String terminated by Null, usually for initialising a (char) Array (see 3.0) whereas `'AB'` only specifies the contents of 2 successive Bytes. Literal Constants using Apostrophe are employed usually in an Assignment of a single ASCII Value to a Numeric Variable, e.g.

```
c = 'A';
```

Quotes, Apostrophes, non-printing Characters and other problematic Byte Values can be specified within a Literal Constant by use of Backslash (\) constructs, see 3.1.5, 3.1.7 and Appendix B.

3.1.1 Make a Variable, Z, contain HALLO
```
char z[] = "HALLO";
```
initialised upon being declared.
(Some Compilers allow this for external Variables only).
or:
```
char *z; ...; z = "HALLO";
```
or:
```
char z[80]; ...; strcpy(z,"HALLO");
```

3.1.2 What is the longest String that can be Assigned?
65535 characters.

3.1.3 Does it matter what Z was before a String Assignment?
Yes, z should be (char *), a pointer to a (char) target.

3.1.4 Make Z contain a single Character, A
```
int z; ...; z = 'A';
```
or:
```
char z; ...; z = 'A';
```
Note that (char) and (int) are equivalent here.

3.1.5 Can non-printable Characters be specified in a String Constant?
Yes, by using the Backslash (\) construct.

3.1.6 Make Z contain Carriage Return (ASCII 13)
```
char c; ...; c = '\r';
```
or:
```
char z[] = "LINE1\rLINE2";
```
Note that for the sake of compatibility, \n (Newline) is generally used instead of \r (Carriage Return) to break lines.

3.1.7 Make Z contain Apostrophe (ASCII 39)
```
char z; ...; z = '\'';
```
or:
```
char z; ...; z = 0x39;
```

3.1.8 Make Z contain Quote (ASCII 34)
```
char z; ...; z = '\"';
```
or:
```
char z; ...; z = 0x34;
```

3.1.9 Make Integer C contain the ASCII code of Asterisk (*)
```
int c; ...; c = '*';
```
Note that '*' is a Constant of Type (int), which is equivalent to (char) here.

In most C implementations `'*'` (Asterisk is ASCII 42) specifies the 16
Bit Pattern:
```
 0000 0000 0010 1010
```
However `"*"` specifies a String Constant yielding (with trailing `'\0'`)
the (2 Byte) Bit Pattern:
```
 0010 1010 0000 0000
```

3.1.10 Make Integer C contain the ASCII code of the Character in Z

```
char z; int c; ...; c = (int) z;
```
or:
```
char *z; int c; ...; c = (int) *z;
```

3.1.11 Make Integer C contain the ASCII code of a single Keystroke

```
c = getch(); /* does not echo the keystroke */
```
or:
```
c = getche(); /* does echo the keystroke */
```

3.1.12 Specify a particular Character by its ASCII code, e.g. 42

```
z = 42;
```

3.1.13 Make Z a String of N repetitions of Asterisk (*)

```
char z[N]; ...; z[N] = '\0'; strset(z,'*');
```
Note that `strset()` needs z to be an existing String of length N.
If your library does not contain `strset()` then use instead:
```
for (i=0; i<N; i++) z[i] = '*';
```

3.1.14 Make Z a String of N Spaces

Use 3.1.13, with `' '` in place of `'*'`.

3.1.15 Print N Spaces between Slashes /.../

```
putchar('/'); for (i=0; i<N; i++) putchar(' ');
   putchar('/');
```
If N is a known Numeral, e.g. 45:
```
printf("/%45s/"," ");
```

3.1.16 Generate a String of length N from repetitions of String S

```
z[0] = '\0';
while (strlen(z)<N) strcat(z,s);
z[N] = '\0';
```
Note that the last call of `strcat(z,s)` may overshoot the N-1th
Character in z.

3.2 String Variables

A String Variable is an Array (Pointer) of Type (char), typically declared:

```
char *z; /* does not allocate space for the
   String */
```

or:

```
char z[N]; /* allocates N+1 Bytes (of garbage)
   for the String */
```

or:

```
char z[] = "HALLO"; /* points z at a valid (6
   Byte) ASCIIZ String */
```

See remarks at 2.8 and 3.0. Typical Program Errors arise from using Functions like strncpy() and forgetting to supply a Null Byte to terminate the String contents (see 3.3.5), or forgetting that a String Variable currently may not point to any meaningful String Value or to sufficient space to write one of the desired length.

3.2.1 Maximum length that a String Variable can attain

Limited only by Memory constraints. In practice 32767 due to Loop counters being declared (int) rather than (size_t) in Functions which manipulate Strings. In Zortech C (size_t) is equivalent to (unsigned) which sets a practical limit of 65535.

3.2.2 Make Integer L contain the current length of String Z

```
l = strlen(z);
```

Note that strlen() returns a (size_t) Number. See 3.2.1.

3.3 Substrings

Unlike most Languages supporting Strings, C contains no String concatenation primitive. Instead the contents of the second String must be copied to the end of the first String, overwriting the terminating Null. Remember to supply a Null Byte at the new end. The standard Functions strcat() and strcpy() ease this operation and look after the Nulls. Both modify (the target of) their first Argument String, but also return a Pointer Value to the finished String. Use strncpy() instead of strcpy() to move just a given number of Bytes (see 3.3.5, 3.3.7) but note that strncpy() does not supply the missing Null (however see 3.3.8).

WARNING: Functions that modify their Arguments (like scanf()) need Pointers to the Variable to be modified, not the Value itself. This is typically achieved by prefixing the Variable Name with the Ampersand (&) Operator. However Strings are already Pointers in effect, so be careful not to write strcpy(&s,u) instead of strcpy(s,u). The former will overwrite Memory capriciously.

3.3.1 Concatenate the String U to the back of String Z
```
strcat(z,u);
```
Allocate sufficient Memory space to the target of z to accommodate u.

3.3.2 Concatenate the String U to the front of String Z
```
z = strcat( strcpy(y,u),z );
```

3.3.3 Drop the first Character from String Z
```
char *z; ...; z++;
```
or:
```
char *p, z[100]; ...; p = z; p++;
```
or:
```
strcpy(z,z+1);
```

3.3.4 Drop the last Character from String Z
```
z[strlen(z)-1] = '\0';
```
simply moves the terminating Null Byte forward.

3.3.5 Make Z the first N Characters from String U
```
char z[100];
...
strncpy(z,u,N);
z[N] = '\0'; /* supplying the Null Byte strncpy()
   omits */
```

3.3.6 Make Z the last N Characters from String U
```
strcpy(z, u+strlen(u)-N);
```

3.3.7 Make Z the N Characters from String U starting with the Jth
```
strncpy(z, u+j-1, N);
z[N] = '\0';
```

3.3.8 What if U contains less than N Characters?
Fewer Characters are copied from u, but final '\0' is copied.

3.3.9 Search for substring U within String Z
```
strsearch(s,u);
...
strsearch(char *s, char *u)
{
 char *p; int n;
 p = s; n = strlen(u);
 while ((*p!='\0')&&strncmp(p,u,n)) p++;
 if (p==(s+strlen(s))) return(0);
 else return(1+(p-s));
}
```

Note that `strsearch()` returns the position of the starting Character of substring u (1 if this is s[0]), or 0 if u not found.

3.3.10 Replace each occurrence of substring U within String Z by substring V

```
strreplace(s,u,v);
...
char *strreplace( char *s, char *u, char *v)
{
char *p; int i, n;
static char t[500]; /* buffer */
 p = s; n = strlen(u); t[0] = '\0';
 while (i = /*assignment*/ strsearch(p,u)) {
   strncat(t,p,i-1);
   p += I+n-1;
   strcat(t,v);
 }
 strcat(t,p); return(t);
}
```

3.3.11 Eliminate trailing Spaces from String Z

```
i = strlen(z)-1; while (z[i]==' ') z[i--] = '\0';
```

3.4 Uppercase/Lowercase conversion

The ANSI standard provides only single-Character translation Functions, `toupper()` and `tolower()`. However Zortech C provides `strupr()` and `strlwr()` which act on whole Strings.

3.4.1 Make Variable Y equal to String Z converted to Uppercase throughout

```
char *y; ...; y = strupr(z);
```
Note that `strupr()` is a non-standard (Zortech) library function.
or:
```
char *y; ...; y=z;
while (*y = /*assignment*/ toupper(*y)) y++;
```

3.4.2 Make Variable Y equal to String Z converted to Lowercase throughout

```
char *y; ...; y = strlwr(z);
```
Note that `strlwr()` is a non-standard (Zortech) library function.
or:
```
char *y; ...; y=z;
while (*y = /*assignment*/ tolower(*y)) y++;
```

3.5 String/Numeric conversion

The standard support for operations to extract the Numeric Value from a Numeral within a String is provided by the range of Functions, atoi(), atof() and atol() in the standard library "stdlib". Somewhat extended facilities are provided by strtod(), strtol() and strtoul() if required, also sprintf(). Assume calls to these Functions are preceded in the Program by:

```
#include <stdlib.h>
```
or, for sprintf():
```
#include <stdio.h>
```

3.5.1 Convert a Number, e.g. 123.56 to a Numeral String

```
char s[50], float n=123.56;
...
sprintf(s,"%f",n);
```

3.5.2 Right-justify the Numeral within a String of length W

```
sprintf(s,"%25f",n);
```
supposing that W is 25.

3.5.3 Convert a String, Z, containing the Numeral 99 to the Integer 99

```
#include <string.h>
...
int i; ...; i = atoi(z);
```

3.5.4 Convert a String containing the Numeral 12.34 to the Non-Integer 12.34

```
#include <string.h>
...
double dd, atof(char[]);
...
dd = atof(z);
```

3.5.5 What if the String consists of Null or Spaces only?

Result is Zero.

3.5.6 What if the String does not contain a valid Numeral?

Leading Spaces are ignored. Conversion continues until Space or the first non-valid Character. Examples:

```
atoi("123X45")==123
```
or:
```
atoi(" 123 45")==123
```
or:
```
atoi("X45")==0
```

3.5.7 Evaluate the Expression contained in a String, Z+1-Y
Not supported in C. The Identifier of a given Variable is not available at Runtime.

3.6 String Arrays

3.6.1 Specify a String Array, A, of N Terms
```
char *a[N];
```
actually an Array of N (char *) Pointers.

3.6.2 Place HALLO in Array, A, as the Term having Index 2
```
a[2] = "HALLO";
```

3.6.3 Make Z Character k in the Term j of String Array, A
```
z = a[j][k];
```

3.7 Code Strings
Since C is a compiled Language, Run-time interpretation of Strings containing C Statements would need access to the Compiler. Zortech C does not support this, nor do any other of the principal vendors' offerings. However the Function system() will Run COM-MAND.COM, taking a given DOS Command as a String Argument. Note that COMMAND.COM is terminated on return from system(), taking its environment with it, so it is no good resetting environment Strings using system().

3.7.1 Execute a literal Statement contained in a String
Not supported in C. The Compiler is not available for Language Syntax processing at Runtime.

3.7.2 What if the String consists of Null or Spaces only?
N/A.

3.7.3 What if the String does not contain a valid Statement?
N/A.

3.7.4 Execute DOS Command, DIR, contained in the String, Z
```
system("DIR");
```
or:
```
system("dir");
```

3.7.5 Verify that the DOS Command Executed successfully
Test the (int) Value returned by system(), which is Zero if COMMAND.COM Ran successfully, otherwise (-1), e.g.
```
if (system(s)) {...}
```
{...} contains the Error action.

4

Display text data on the Screen

C supports the task of writing Numbers to the Screen, embedded in a textual message, primarily by means of printf(), a tricky but powerful Function in the standard library "stdio". The first Argument of printf() is the "format" String, usually a Literal Constant in Quotes. At its simplest the format String is printed as a message. However, optionally embedded in the format String are "conversion specifications" each beginning with the reserved escape Character Percent (%) and ending with a "conversion character" (one of a set of Letters). Each succeeding conversion specification causes printf() to look for a succeeding Argument (following the first) and embed its (converted) Value in the output message at the point indicated by the Percent. How printf() handles that Argument (e.g. as a Number or a Pointer) depends entirely on the corresponding conversion specification and not at all on the Type of the actual Argument, which you must ensure matches the conversion specification's requirements.

A format String is mandatory with printf() even if only Numbers are to be printed. In this case it consists just of one conversion specification per additional Argument, padded with Spaces as required.

4.1 Display message containing a Number

This section considers how to display Numbers embedded in Literal Constants.

4.1.1 Display a single Value, X, containing e.g. 99
```
int x; ...; printf("%d",x);
```

4.1.2 Display X as THE ANSWER IS 99
```
int x; ...; printf("THE ANSWER IS %d",x);
```

4.1.3 Display X as THE ANSWER IS 99 SECONDS
```
int x; ...; printf("THE ANSWER IS %d SECONDS",x);
```

4.2 Display a formatted Number

4.2.1 Print X within 7 Character Field, to 2 decimal places (e.g. 9999.99)
```
double x; ...; printf("%7.2f",x);
```

4.2.2 What if X takes more than 7 Characters? (e.g. -9999.99)
Field is widened sufficiently to accommodate the Number.

4.2.3 What range of X will fit into a 7 Character Field?
-999.99 thru 9999.99.

4.3 Display several Numbers in a row
This section considers how to display a row of Numbers, then spaced to
fall in columns, then how to add column headings to match the spacing.

4.3.1 Display a row of Integers, W, X, Y, Z
```
printf("%d %d %d %d",w,x,y,z);
```

**4.3.2 Tabulate successive Integers, J, K, L, M, in columns 7
Characters wide**
```
printf("%7d%7d%7d%7d",j,k,l,m);
```

4.3.3 What if a row is too long for the Screen?
It gets wrapped around to the following Screen line.

**4.3.4 Print header text to label the columns RED YELLOW
GREEN BLUE**
```
printf("%7s%7s%7s%7s","RED","YELLOW",
  "GREEN","BLUE");
```
The header Strings will be left-justified in their fields.

4.4 Tabulate a Numeric Array

**4.4.1 Tabulate a 4 by 4 Numeric Array, A, in column widths
chosen by the System**
```
for (i=0; i<4; i++) {
 for (j=0; j<4; j++) printf("%f",a[i][j]);
 putchar('\n');
 }
```

**4.4.2 Tabulate a 4 by 4 Numeric Array, A, to 2 decimal places
in columns 7 Characters wide**
```
for (i=0; i<4; i++) {
 for (j=0; j<4; j++) printf("%7.2f",a[i][j]);
 putchar('\n');
 }
```

4.5 Display coloured text on the Screen

The ANSI standard libraries do not include any Functions to handle coloured Screens. Zortech C contains a set of device-dependent Functions to handle the CGA and EGA Screen devices efficiently. Their Identifiers all begin with: disp ... These Functions are capable of placing coloured text where required on the Screen.

4.5.1 Display the text PRESS ENTER in the centre of the Screen in white upon blue Field 13 Characters wide

```
#include<disp.h>
...
disp_open();
disp_move(12,33);
disp_setattr(0x17); /* white upon blue */
disp_printf(" PRESS ENTER ");
```

4.5.2 Display a full width bright red line 24 with ERROR MESSAGE in yellow placed centrally

```
#include<disp.h>
...
disp_open();
disp_setattr(0x4E); /* yellow upon red */
disp_move(24,0); disp_printf("%79c",' ');
   disp_move(24,33);
disp_printf("ERROR MESSAGE");
```
79 must be used instead of 80 to avoid bottom line being scrolled.

4.5.3 Display ERROR MESSAGE in blinking yellow placed centrally on line 24

As 4.5.2 but with:
```
disp_setattr(0xEE); /* blinking yellow upon red */
```

4.5.4 Restore white Characters upon black background

```
#include<disp.h>
...
disp_open();
...
disp_setattr(0x07);
```
or:
```
disp_setattr(DISP_NORMAL);
```
See <disp.h> for other useful attribute Constants.

4.6 Confine scrolling text input/output to part of the Screen only

Freezing lines on the Screen and leaving other parts scrollable is not directly supported in C. You must handle the scrolling and storage of displayed lines yourself. Likewise a Window facility is not directly supported by the basic Zortech C (although Function libraries to do this can be purchased from Zortech or other vendors). Failing these you must program a Window explicitly using the disp_ Functions (see 4.6.7).

4.6.1 Purpose
To provide a text Window facility, whereby existing text can be "frozen" on the Screen outside a conversational Window, undisturbed by any ensuing conversation in that Window.

4.6.2 Confine conversation to the top line only
Not supported in C.

4.6.3 Confine conversation to the bottom 2 lines only
Not supported in C.

4.6.4 Confine conversation to the upper 12 lines of the Screen
Not supported in C.

4.6.5 Confine conversation to the lower 12 lines of the Screen
Not supported in C.

4.6.6 Restore conversation to the whole Screen
Not supported in C.

4.6.7 Superimpose a text Window (white upon blue) 3 Rows, 60 Columns, starting in Row 5, Column 10
```
#include<disp.h>
int i;
...
disp_open();
...
disp_setattr(0x17); /* white upon blue */
for (i=0; i<3; i++) {
disp_move(i+4,9);
disp_printf("%60c",' ');
}
```

4.6.8 Display an Asterisk in upper left corner of this Window
```
#include<disp.h>
...
disp_open();
```

```
...
disp_move(4,9); disp_putc('*');
```

4.6.9 Remove the text Window, restoring the text underneath

Not supported in C. You must save and restore the Screen contents
yourself.

5

Draw graphics on the Screen

Graphics support is not specified by the ANSI standard. Different
vendors are therefore at liberty to support PC graphics in a
Hardware-dependent and idiosyncratic way.

Zortech C comes with the "fg" graphics library (standing for "flash
graphics"). All Functions and other public Identifiers in this library begin
with: fg_ ... In what follows, assume calls to these Functions are
preceded in the Program by:
```
#include <fg.h>
```

Two alternative libraries are provided, FG and FGDEBUG. The latter
contains Error detection code calling _assert() and is the recommended one during development. Once the Program is finalised, substituting
the FG library during linking will give slightly better efficiency.

5.1 The various graphics modes supported

"fg" recognises most graphics boards for the PC. The Function
fg_init_all() automatically configures at compile-time for the
installed board, e.g. CGA, EGA, VGA, Hercules or Toshiba 3100 plasma
(near-VGA). However the board type can be overridden at Run-time by
altering the DOS environment string FG_DISPLAY. Inspect the contents
of File FG.H for the various options if you think you need to do this.

5.1.1 Set Screen to medium resolution graphics mode
```
if (fg_init_cgamedres()==FG_NULL) exit(1);
```

5.1.2 Set Screen to high resolution graphics mode
```
if (fg_init_all()==FG_NULL) exit(1);
```

fg_init_all() attempts to discover the type of graphics board installed and configures the System accordingly.

5.1.3 Restore Screen to 80-column monochrome text mode
```
fg_term();
```
Note that `fg_init()` will then restore the previously set-up graphics mode if required.

5.2 Built-in Functions and Screen Coordinates

"Built-in" is here understood to mean: provided by the "fg" library. Most of the usual graphics figures can be drawn with a single `fg_...` Function call. A single Argument (generally the 4th or 5th) specifies the coordinates of the line or box concerned. This may take a range of forms for which separate Types are provided (see 5.2.2). A few Functions (e.g. `fg-drawdot()`, see 5.3.1) employ separate x- and y- Arguments.

5.2.1 What facilities relate to graphics?

Those Identifiers which are declared in the File `FG.H`. Specifically the read-only Variables initialised by `fg_init_all()`:

```
fg_displaybox fg_charbox fg_ncolormap
fg_nsimulcolor fg_pixelx fg_pixely fg_numpages
fg_display fg_activepage fg_displaypage
```

and the Functions:

```
_assert() fg_lineclip() fg_adjustxy() fg_blit()
fg_box_cpy() fg_drawarc() fg_drawbox()
fg_drawdot() fg_drawellipse() fg_drawline()
fg_drawlinep() fg_drawlineclip() fg_drawmatrix()
fg_drawthickline() fg_fill() fg_fillbox()
fg_flush() fg_getcolormap() fg_init_null()
fg_init_all() fg_init_egaecd()
```
(...**and** relatives for various graphics boards)
```
fg_line_cpy() fg_putc() fg_puts()
fg_readbox() fg_readdot() fg_restore() fg_save()
fg_setactivepage() fg_setcolormap()
fg_setdisplaypage() fg_setlinepattern() fg_term()
fg_writebox().
```

5.2.2 What comprise (x,y) Coordinates in a graphics Statement?

(1) Two consecutive (Integer) Arguments in certain Function calls, e.g. Variables x, y, each of Type: `fg_coord_t`. This is defined in FG.H as:
```
typedef int fg_coord_t;
```
(2) A 4-Term Array of Type: `fg_line_t`, representing two pairs of Coordinates standing for the end-points of a Straight Line. This is

defined in FG.H as:
```
 typedef fg_coord_t[4] fg_line_t;
```
(3) A Pointer to a Straight Line Value as in (2) above. This is defined in FG.H as:
```
 typedef fg_coord_t *fg_pline_t;
```
(4) A 4-Term Array of Type: fg_box_t, representing two pairs of Coordinates standing for the (lower left, upper right) corners of a Box. This is defined in FG.H as:
```
 typedef fg_coord_t[4] fg_box_t;
```
(5) A Pointer to a Box Value as in (4) above. This is defined in FG.H as:
```
 typedef fg_coord_t *fg_pbox_t;
```

5.2.3 Does the first Coordinate refer to horizontal distance?
Yes.

5.2.4 Where is Point (0,0) on the Screen?
Lower left.

5.2.5 What are the Coordinates of the diagonally opposite corner of the Screen?
```
 fg_displaybox[FG_X2], fg_displaybox[FG_Y2].
```
For a standard CGA high resolution Screen this is equivalent to 639,199.
However the programmer is recommended to use these symbolic Constants and public Variables, as defined in FG.H, instead of explicit Numerals.

5.3 Points, Lines and other graphic figures

Separate Functions are provided to draw Points, Straight Lines, hollow and filled Boxes and Ellipses. All are parameterised by Arguments (1, 2 and 3) to specify colour, writing mode (XOR or overwrite) and Bit-plane Mask. In the following examples these are chosen simply to overwrite whatever is already there with white lines. Another Argument (4) is sometimes offered to determine line-type (solid, dotted, etc., see 5.3.2 - 5.3.4). Set this to a choice of #defined Constant appearing in File FG.H. These all begin with: FG_LINE...

One significant feature of Zortech's "fg" is the ability to adjust an Ellipse to be circular automatically, whatever the actual installed graphics board happens to be, by scaling it with the known Pixel height and width (see 5.3.7).

5.3.1 Brighten a single Pixel at Point (x=200, y=100)
```
 x = 200; y = 100;
 fg_drawdot(FG_WHITE, FG_MODE_SET, ~0, x, y);
```

5.3.2 Draw a Straight Line from upper left corner to lower right corner of the Screen

```
fg_line_t myline;
...
myline[FG_X1] = fg_displaybox[FG_X2];
myline[FG_Y1] = fg_displaybox[FG_Y1];
myline[FG_X2] = fg_displaybox[FG_X1];
myline[FG_Y2] = fg_displaybox[FG_Y2];
fg_drawline(FG_WHITE, FG_MODE_SET, ~0,
  FG_LINE_SOLID, myline);
```

5.3.3 Draw a Straight Line from Point (x,y) to Point (u=300, v=150)

```
myline[FG_X1] = x;
myline[FG_Y1] = y;
myline[FG_X2] = u = 300;
myline[FG_Y2] = v = 150;
fg_drawline(FG_WHITE, FG_MODE_SET, ~0,
  FG_LINE_SOLID, myline);
```

5.3.4 Draw a hollow Box from Point (x,y) to Point (u,v)

```
mybox[FG_X1] = x;
mybox[FG_Y1] = y;
mybox[FG_X2] = u;
mybox[FG_Y2] = v;
fg_drawbox(FG_WHITE, FG_MODE_SET, ~0,
  FG_LINE_SOLID, mybox, fg_displaybox);
```

5.3.5 Draw a filled Box from Point (x,y) to Point (u,v)

```
fg_fillbox(FG_WHITE, FG_MODE_SET, ~0, mybox);
```
Assume mybox as in 5.3.4.

5.3.6 Draw a quadrilateral (Polyline) through Points (a=250, b=50), (c=350, d=40), (e=400, f=180), (g=200, h=150)

```
fg_coord_t quad[] = {250,50, 350,40, 400,180,
  200,150, 250,50};
...
polyline(quad, sizeof quad); /*draw polyline:
  quad */
...
void polyline( fg_coord_t *shape, int n )
/* general routine to draw a polyline of any
  length */
{
int i; fg_line_t nextline;
n = (n/4)-1; /*n is now no.of lines to draw*/
```

```
for (i=0; i<n; i++) {
  fg_line_cpy( nextline, shape+i+i );
  fg_drawline( FG_WHITE, FG_MODE_SET, ~0,
    FG_LINE_SOLID, nextline);
  }
}
```

5.3.7 Draw a Circle of radius R=50 centred on Point (x,y)

```
fg_drawarc(FG_WHITE, FG_MODE_SET, ~0, x,y, 50,
  0,3600, fg_displaybox);
```

This is a Circle in the sense of being 100 Pixels both wide and high, but on many Screens this will not appear circular. Instead try drawing an Ellipse with x- and y-radii in the ratio: (fg_pixelx:fg_pixely):

```
fg_drawellipse(FG_WHITE, FG_MODE_SET, ~0, x,y,
  50,50*fg_pixelx/fg_pixely, 0,3600,
  fg_displaybox);
```

5.4 Shades and colours

All Functions to draw a graphic figure take an Argument to specify the colour to be used. You should use the Named Constants provided in FG.H (see 5.4.2) rather than the corresponding Numerals (see 5.4.1).

5.4.1 Fill a graphic shape with colour number 1

```
fg_fill(x,y, FG_BLUE, FG_WHITE);
```

Assume that x,y are Coordinates within the closed boundary of the graphic shape, which has been drawn in white.
FG_BLUE is defined to be 1. See 5.4.2.

5.4.2 Specify Named Constants for BLACK, BLUE, GREEN, CYAN, RED, MAGENTA, BROWN, WHITE, BRIGHT, YELLOW

Corresponding Identifiers have already been #defined in FG.H and should be used instead. They are:
FG_BLACK FG_BLUE FG_GREEN FG_CYAN FG_BLUE_GREEN
FG_RED FG_MAGENTA FG_PURPLE FG_YELLOW FG_WHITE
FG_GRAY FG_LIGHT_BLUE FG_LIGHT_GREEN
FG_LIGHT_CYAN FG_LIGHT_BLUE_GREEN FG_LIGHT_RED
FG_LIGHT_MAGENTA FG_YELLOW FG_BROWN
FG_LIGHT_WHITE FG_HIGHLIGHT FG_BLINK.

5.4.3 Change colour of background to blue

```
fg_fillbox(FG_BLUE, FG_MODE_SET, ~0,
  fg_displaybox);
```

has the meaning: clear the whole Screen by filling outer frame boundary with blue.

5.4.4 Change colour of background to bright blue
```
fg_fillbox(FG_LIGHT_BLUE, FG_MODE_SET, ~0,
   mybox);
```

5.4.5 Change colour of foreground to red
```
fg_drawline( FG_RED, FG_MODE_SET, ~0,
   FG_LINE_SOLID, myline);
```

5.4.6 Change colour of background to black and foreground to white
```
fg_fillbox(FG_BLACK, FG_MODE_SET, ~0, mybox);
fg_drawline( FG_WHITE, FG_MODE_SET, ~0,
   FG_LINE_SOLID, myline);
```

5.5 Animation

The Pixel settings within a given rectangular area on the Screen may be saved in a String or other allocated Memory space, a, using fg_readbox() and written back using fg_writebox() to the same place (to erase the figure, see 5.5.3) then elsewhere. The Function fg_blit() is also provided to move rectangular areas rapidly within or between Screen pages (see 5.5.4).

5.5.1 Capture a graphic image from the Screen into Variable A
```
fg_color_t *a;
...
a = (fg_color_t *) malloc(N);
fg_readbox(mybox, a);
```
Assume that mybox (e.g. as specified in 5.3.4) surrounds the image to be captured. Note that N must be chosen to be sufficiently large, viz. an Integer for each Pixel stored.

5.5.2 Transfer a graphic image stored in Variable A to the Screen
```
fg_writebox(newbox, a);
```
The Variable newbox must have the same Type and dimensions as mybox (see 5.5.1), but can be anywhere on the Screen.

5.5.3 Erase a graphic image
For a graphic image written by means of calls having the (2nd) Argument: FG_MODE_SET, writing the image a second time with FG_MODE_XOR will erase it.
Otherwise suppose the image is surrounded by mybox (see 5.3.4):
```
fg_handle_t savearea;
...
```

```
savearea = fg_save(mybox);
/* now draw the image */
...
fg_restore(savearea); /*erase the image*/
```

5.5.4 Move a graphic image from Point (x,y) to Point (p,q)

Adapt 5.5.1 and 5.5.2.

Alternatively (avoiding use of a storage Variable):

```
fg_blit(mybox, p,q, 0,0);
```

Assume `mybox` is as in 5.3.4.

Clipping to the boundary, `fg_displaybox`, is not done by this Function, so that `p,q` must be chosen with care.

The last two Arguments are source page and target page, both being page Zero in this case.

6

Error handling at Runtime

C provides very patchy Error diagnosis and handling. In many respects C Programs are as hard to debug as Assembler Programs. Errors are best avoided rather than cured by using those facilities of the Language, e.g. the preprocessor, Type-checking and structured constructs, which minimise error-proneness.

Limited Error detection and analysis is supported by the Function `assert()` (which needs `#include <assert.h>`) and the external Variable `errno`. Mathematical Functions can be furnished with a Function `matherr()` (see 6.3.2). This sort of Error arises when a library Function gets called with an inappropriate Value in an Argument and can be trapped under Program control. More fundamental Errors will cause malfunction at the machine code level, from which C offers no way to recover.

6.1 Report a Program Error

6.1.1 Discover the source Statement at which the Error occurred

Syntax Errors are located and diagnosed during Compilation with the aid of the ZED Editor. For locating Run-time Errors, the programmer should use the Zortech debugger, or MS-Codeview, which operate with the Runtime Application. Compiling code with the flag: -g inserts line numbers into the actual object File.

6.1.2 Diagnose the Error

Not supported in C for Statements in general.

See the remarks at 6.1.1. However, many library Functions place a Value in the external Integer Variable: errno.

Limited diagnosis is possible by:

```
#include<assert.h>
...
assert(X!=Y);
```

If (X!=Y) is Zero (False), Program will abort with the message:

```
Assertion failure: "X!=Y" on line 123 in file
        myprog.c
```

The Statement X!=Y can be replaced by any Integer Expression.

6.2 Report a Device Error

6.2.1 Diagnose the type of Device Error

Not generally supported in C. Occurrence of a File Error can be detected and acted-upon by inspecting the error flag for the given stream (or File) as follows:

```
#include<stdio.h>
...
FILE *f;
...
if (ferror(f)) {
 clearerr(f);
 /* perform diagnostic checks... */
 ...
 }
```

6.3 Recover from Error

6.3.1 Execute a given Statement when any sort of Program Error occurs

Not generally supported in C. If Error permits _exit() to be called:

```
void mystatement(void); /* your Subroutine to
  call on exit */
...
atexit(mystatement);
...
```

6.3.2 Execute given Statement when a given Program Error occurs, then continue the Run

Not generally supported in C. If the Error is of a kind which sets a non-Zero Value in the Variable errno, then errno can be tested in a conditional Statement. See chapter 7.

In Zortech C the Functions in the library "math" call a Function: matherr(), which you can optionally supply. To handle a particular type of Error, e.g. DOMAIN Error:

```c
#include <math.h>
...
int matherr(xxx)
struct exception *xxx; /* declared in <math.h> */
{
  if (xxx->type==DOMAIN) {
    /* required Statement should go here */
    return(0);
  }
  else return(1);
}
```

6.3.3 Disable Error trapping under Program control

Not generally supported in C. The Function: assert() can be disabled by inserting the following line at the head of the Program:

```c
#define NDEBUG
```

6.4 Trace Program Execution

Not supported in C. Use a proprietary debugger, see 6.1.1. Setting the -g switch during Compilation inserts line number information in the object File to aid the location of faulty Statements in the source Program.

7

Execute a Statement conditionally or repetitively

This chapter embraces everything to do with Branching, Looping and flow of control. C provides good support for structured Programs with the use of Braces { ... } to gather sequences of Statements into Blocks which can be employed wherever a simple Statement might occur (and vice versa). However the structured discipline imposed by Braces { ... } can be evaded, e.g. with the `goto` and `case/break` constructs.

C supports Conditional Execution with the `if` and `if/else` constructs, also `switch/case/break/default`. C supports repetitive Execution with `for` (see 7.9.3) `while` (see 7.9.16) and `do/while` (see 7.9.17). All these constructs make use of Conditions, which are Numeric Expressions having Logical force. Any non-Zero Value for the Condition is treated as True (see 7.6.1).

Complete support is provided for simple and complex Conditions, but note the unique Syntax for certain conventional Logical operators (see 7.4). Particularly confusing for the novice is the use of `==` for Logical comparison (see 7.3.5). Equals (`=`) always means Assignment and multiple Assignments can occur in a single (simple) Statement. In fact any sub-Expression can become the object of an incidental Assignment. For example, in the Conditional Statement:

```
if (a=5) z+=1;
```

the Condition (`a=5`) is effectively (`5`) which is always True since it is non-Zero, therefore `z` always gets incremented. In the course of evaluating the Condition, `a` gets Assigned the Value `5`. What this Statement does NOT do is compare `a` with `5` to determine whether or not to increment `z`. This feature is the source of many subtle bugs. See also 7.5.1.

7.1 What constitutes a Statement?

A Statement can be any simple or compound Statement in C. As typical examples of simple Statements we shall use:

```
z+=1;
```

or a simple Subroutine Invocation:

```
mysub();
```

As a typical example of a compound Statement, or Block { ... } we shall use:

```
{
z+=1;
printf("%d",z);
}
```

7.2 What constitutes a Condition?

A Condition can be any Numeric Expression. If this evaluates to Zero then we shall say the Condition is False, otherwise it is True. Usually however a Condition is a Logical or Boolean Expression. Such

Expressions result in Truth-Values which happen to be the Integers: 0 (for False), 1 (for True). Compound Conditions are built up from simple Conditions by Logical Operators, `&&`, `||`, etc.

As typical examples of Conditions we shall use:

```
(a<5)
```
or:
```
(y>10)
```
or:
```
((a<5)||(y>10))
```

Examples of Conditions in Statements:
```
if (a<5) z+=1;
```
or:
```
if (y>10) z+=1; else z+=3;
```
or:
```
b = (a<5);
```

7.3 The repertoire of simple Conditions

Simple Conditions are formed by infix Logical Operators which apply between Numbers and Pointers. String comparison is not a C primitive but is provided by the standard library Functions `strcmp()` and `strcmpl()`. Assume for these:
```
#include <string.h>
```
Note the remarks about `(a=5)` and `(a==5)` in 7.0. See also 7.3.5.

7.3.1 A is less than 5
```
(a<5)
```

7.3.2 A is not less than 5 (i.e. A is greater than or equal to 5)
```
(a>=5)
```

7.3.3 A is greater than 5
```
(a>5)
```

7.3.4 A is not greater than 5 (i.e. A is less than or equal to 5)
```
(a<=5)
```

7.3.5 A is equal to 5
```
(a==5)
```
WARNING: Be sure to use the Logical Operator `==` and not the Assignment Operator `=`, since `(a=5)` is nevertheless a valid Condition, assigning 5 to Variable a and then signifying True (because a is non-Zero).

7.3.6 A is not equal to 5
```
(a!=5)
```

7.3.7 Character CH is Y
```
char ch;
...
(ch=='Y')
```

7.3.8 Character CH is not Y
```
char ch;
...
(ch!='Y')
```

7.3.9 Character CH precedes Y in System-determined order
```
char ch;
...
(ch<'Y')
```
the ASCII codes of ch and 'Y' being compared.

7.3.10 String S is HALLO
```
( strcmp(s,"HALLO")==0 )
```
or:
```
( strcmpl(s,"HALLO")==0 )
```
strcmpl() ignores upper/lowercase differences.
Variable s may be declared as:
```
char *s;
```
or:
```
char s[N]; /* N being an Integer Constant */
```
or:
```
char s[] = "any given string";
```

7.3.11 String S precedes HALLO in System-determined order
```
( strcmp(s,"HALLO")<0 )
```
or:
```
( strcmpl(s,"HALLO")<0 )
```
See 7.3.10.

7.3.12 String S is empty (Null)
```
( strlen(s)==0 )
```
or:
```
( s[0]=='\0' )
```
exploiting the fact that the Null Character always terminates a conventional C String.

7.3.13 String S begins with HALLO
```
( strncmp(S,"HALLO",5)==0 )
```

7.3.14 Error Conditions
```
(errno)
```
The actual Value of errno helps diagnose the Error.

7.3.15 Timer Conditions
N/A

7.3.16 Hardware Conditions
N/A

7.3.17 File Conditions
```
#include<stdio.h>
FILE *f;

...
( feof(f) )
```
or:
```
( ferror(f) ) /* see 6.2.1. */
```
or:
```
( fflush(f) )
```

7.4 Form a compound Condition, a logical combination of simple Conditions

Unlike some Languages (e.g. BASIC) there are separate sets of Logical and Bitwise Operators. Ampersand (&) and Bar (|) are Bitwise Operators acting upon Bit Patterns and returning Bit Patterns (see 7.6.4). The Logical Operators AND and OR are && and || respectively (see 7.4.1, 7.4.2). These return 1 (True) or 0 (False) only.

Throughout this section assume a, b, c, d are declared as (int), and that b, c contain the results of Conditions, being either True (1) or False (0).

7.4.1 AND
```
(b && c)
```
or:
```
((a<5)&&(y>10))
```

7.4.2 OR
```
(b || c)
```
or:
```
((a<5)||(y>10))
```

7.4.3 NOT
```
!b
```
or:
```
!(a<5)
```

7.4.4 NAND
```
!(b&&c)
```

WARNING: The Parentheses are necessary, otherwise:
```
!b&&c
```
will be interpreted as:
```
(!b)&&c
```

7.4.5 NOR
```
!(b||c)
```
See the above WARNING for NAND.

7.4.6 OR (Exclusive-OR)
Only as a bitwise Operator. Use it if you can be sure b and c can contain only the values 0 or 1 (e.g. as the result of a logical expression):
```
b^c
```
However the following construct simulates a Boolean XOR. !!b is Zero if b is Zero, otherwise it is 1.
```
!!b^!!c
```

7.4.7 Other built-in Logical Operators
There are a separate set of bitwise Operators, which act independently upon corresponding Bits in the two given Integer Values.
```
b&c /* b AND c */
b|c /* b OR c */
b^c /* b XOR c */
```
The following flips all Bits in b (bitwise-NOT):
```
~b
```
The following shifts Bits in b left by c places (b*(2 to power of c)):
```
b<<c
```
The following shifts Bits in b right by c places (b/(2 to power of c)):
```
b>>c
```

7.5 Execute a Statement provided a given Condition is True
Note that C permits some extremely tricky Conditional Assignments. The if construct is employed in 7.5.1 because the intention is to illustrate the most general kind of Conditional Statement. However C permits Conditional Assignments without the use of if. Some C programmers might prefer to use instead:
```
z+=(a<5);
```
relying upon (a<5) evaluating to 0 or 1, or:
```
z+=(a<5)?1:0;
```
The ?/: construct is best used for its chaining property in tasks like the following:
```
z = (a<5)?u : (a==5)?v : w;
```
where z becomes u if a<5, or v if a==5, or w otherwise.

7.5.1 If A is less than 5 then increase Z by 1
```
if (a<5) z+=1;
```

7.5.2 If Y is greater than 10 then increase Z by 1, otherwise increase Z by 3
```
if (y>10) z+=1; else z+=3;
```

7.6 Use True and False as data Values

This should be undertaken with care. Subtle bugs may arise, masked by the acceptance of any non-Zero Value as a True Condition. This section treats the Assignment and display of True/False Values and setting them as individual Bits in an Integer.

7.6.1 Do True and False correspond to Numbers?

Yes. True is 1, False is 0.
In conditional Expressions, any Integer can serve as a Condition, in which case Zero signifies False and non-Zero signifies True.

7.6.2 Are True and False built-in as Logical Constants?

No. If you want to write TRUE and FALSE in your Program, you can define them as symbolic Constants by using the following construct at the head of the Program or in a header File:
```
#define TRUE 1
#define FALSE 0
```

7.6.3 Save the Logical Value (True or False) in a Variable
```
b = 1;
```
or:
```
b = 0;
```

7.6.4 Set Bit 1 of Variable Y to 1 if Condition C is True, otherwise set it to 0.
```
#define MASK 0x4000
...
y = (y&~MASK)|(MASK*!!c);
```

You might want to do this in order to control the individual Bits of a parallel I/O port. Some C implementations allow Bit-Fields, in which individual Bits can be Indexed, but the following is a Masking construct. 0x4000 is the Mask for Bit 1 (counting the leftmost Bit as Bit 0) viz:
```
0100 0000 0000 0000
```

The principle can be extended to other Bits or combinations of Bits by selecting a different MASK.

7.6.5 Make Variable C True if Bit 1 of Variable Y is 1, otherwise make C False

```
c = !!(y&0x4000);
```

The Parentheses are necessary here. Preceding `!!` is (optionally) used to force a non-Zero Value to become 1.

7.6.6 If Bit 1 of Variable Y is 1 then increase Z by 1

```
if (y&0x4000) z+=1;
```

This relies on `if (...)` accepting any non-Zero Value as True.

7.6.7 Display the (True/False) result of a Condition

These constructs just print 0 or 1:

```
printf("%d",c);
```

or:

```
printf("%d",a<5);
```

This construct prints `TRUE` or `FALSE`:

```
if (c) puts("TRUE"); else puts("FALSE");
```

7.7 Execute some other Statement than the next one down

Compound Statements `{...}` and the `if/else` construct remove much of the need to Branch explicitly to a given Statement in order to achieve "intelligent" or "adaptive" Program behaviour. However C does permit Branching as, say, BASIC understands it, and the `case` construct allows Conditional Execution of the Nth Statement in a given list, Indexed by some Integer `N`, thus avoiding the need for chained `if/else` constructs.

7.7.1 The repertoire of Statement Labels

A Statement Label can be any valid Identifier. See 15.1.3.
In what follows, `lab` and `lab2` will be used as typical Labels.

7.7.2 Branch to a Labelled Statement unconditionally

```
goto lab;
...
lab: z+=1;
```

Note that good C programming practice relies on structured constructs using Blocks of Statements `{...}` and avoids `goto`, except perhaps for Error-termination.

7.7.3 Skip the next Statement conditionally

Only by branching to a labelled Statement. See 7.7.4.

7.7.4 Branch to a Labelled Statement conditionally

```
if (a<5) goto lab;
```

```
...
lab: z+=1;
```
See note at 7.7.2 concerning use of `goto`.

7.7.5 Execute the Nth of a choice of Statements

```
int n;
...
switch (n)
{
case 1: z+=1; printf("%d",z); break;
case 2: z+=3; printf("%d",z); break;
case 3: z+=5; printf("%d",z); break;
case 4: z+=7; printf("%d",z); break;
default: printf("%d",z);
}
```

Numeric or Character Constants are permissible as `case` Labels. Typically these are symbolic Constants specified by `#define` or `enum`.

The Label: `default:` can be omitted, in which case no operation takes place if the Value of N fails to match any `case` Label.

```
char ch;
...
switch (ch)
{
case 'a': z+=1; printf("%d",z); break;
case 'b': z+=3; printf("%d",z); break;
case 'c': z+=5; printf("%d",z); break;
case 'd': z+=7; printf("%d",z); break;
}
```

The Statement: `break;` immediately preceding `}` is redundant, but assists Program maintenance.

7.8 Execute a given Statement whenever an Event occurs

Not generally supported in C. The occurrence of an Event cannot by itself trigger a branch to a designated Statement. The Event must first be detected by a Function Invocation, which may serve as the Condition in a Conditional Statement.

Exceptions to this are provided by `matherr()`, see 6.3.2, and by use of the Zortech interrupt handling package in library "int".

7.9 Execute a Statement repeatedly

C has good support for repeated Execution of Statements, or Blocks (which are treated as compound Statements). Backward Conditional Branching is to be discouraged, e.g.

```
if (a<5) goto loop;
```

Instead use:

```
do {...} while (a<5);
```

which tests the Condition only after once performing {...},
or else:

```
while (a<5) {...}
```

which tests the Condition before performing {...} at all.

The construct:

```
for (aaa; bbb; ccc) {...}
```

is much more powerful than most Languages provide in the way of a counter-controlled Loop. The general meaning is as follows:

(1) aaa is performed once at the start of the Loop;

(2) bbb is evaluated (as with while (bbb)) BEFORE each cycle, stopping the Loop if it becomes Zero (False);

(3) ccc is performed once AFTER each cycle of {...}.

7.9.3 illustrates the commonest idiom for stepping i from 0 through 9. Note however that both aaa and ccc can each consist of a list of Expressions (including Assignments), separated by Commas, e.g.

```
for (i=0, j=1, k=k0; i<10; i++, j+=k*k, k++) {...}
```

Often all of the Loop processing can be done within the Parentheses, omitting the trailing Block {...}.

7.9.1 Are compound Statements (Blocks) possible?

Yes. Any number of Statements can be bracketed between Braces {}. Such Blocks can be nested. By convention, Left Brace ({) and Right Brace (}) are followed by line breaks, thus:

```
{
z+=1;
printf("%d",z);
}
```

but the following Syntax is also correct:

```
{z+=1; printf("%d",z);}
```

WARNING: for Pascal programmers: in the foregoing Statement the Semicolon (;) before Right Brace (}) cannot be omitted. It is not a Separator but a Terminator, being part of the actual Statement.

In the samples below, {...} will be used to represent any Statement, simple or compound. If there is only one Statement inside, then the Braces may be omitted. Thus these constructs are equivalent:

```
{z+=1;}
z+=1;
```

7.9.2 Loop forever
```
while (1) {...}
```

7.9.3 Execute a Statement 10 times
```
for (i=0; i<10; i++) {...}
```
A count Variable, i, is necessary here.

7.9.4 Execute a Statement X times
```
for (i=0; i<X; i++) {...}
```
A count Variable, i, is necessary here.

7.9.5 What if X is Zero?
Statement is NOT Executed at all.

7.9.6 What if X is Negative?
Statement is NOT Executed at all.

7.9.7 What if X is a Non-Integer?
X is effectively TRUNCATED (rounded down) to an Integer.

7.9.8 Execute a Statement X times whilst stepping Variable I
```
for (i=1; i<=X; i++) {...}
```
This construct ensures that i takes the Values: 1, 2, 3, ... 10.

7.9.9 Execute a Statement (four times) whilst stepping Variable I from 3 through 6
```
for (i=3; i<=6; i++) {...}
```

7.9.10 Execute a Statement (four times) whilst stepping Variable I from 3 through 20 in steps of 5
```
for (i=3; i<=20; i+=5) {...}
```

7.9.11 Execute a Statement whilst stepping DOWN Variable I from 20 through 3 in steps of X
```
for (i=20; i>=3; i-=X) {...}
```

7.9.12 What if X is Zero?
Loops forever. Can be stopped by {Ctl-Break}.

7.9.13 What if X is Negative (to step in wrong direction)?
Loops forever. Can be stopped by {Ctl-Break}.

7.9.14 What if X is a Non-Integer?
X is effectively ROUNDED UP to the nearest Integer. E.g. X==4.7 would behave like 5. The construct does in fact work (in Zortech C) without needing to re-cast X as (int) X. This is because, supposing X==4.7, X behaves like 4 in the construct:

```
 i+=X;
```
but X behaves like 5 in the construct:
```
 i-=X;
```

7.9.15 Execute a Statement X*Y times whilst stepping Variable I (to X) within Variable J (to Y)
```
for (i=1; i<=X; i++) for (j=1; j<=Y; j++) {...}
```
The following construct is more formal, also more versatile:
```
for (i=1; i<=X; i++)
  {
  for (j=1; j<=Y; j++)
    {
    z+=1;
    printf("%d",z);
    }
  }
```

7.9.16 Execute a Statement, repeating if and only if a given Condition is True
```
do {...} while (a<5);
```
or more formally (notice the final Semicolon):
```
do
 {
  z+=1;
  printf("%d",z);
 }
while (a<5);
```

7.9.17 Repeatedly check a given Condition until it is False, executing a Statement each time it is True
```
while (a<5) {...}
```

8

File and DOS management within an Application

This chapter treats the tasks of disk housekeeping, dealing only with Files which are not Open. Opening, reading and writing Files are treated in Chapter 12.

Zortech C provides system() as the most flexible way of interfacing with DOS. However in analogy with UNIX facilities, unlink() and rename() are provided for erasing and renaming Files. These should be used instead of system() if Program portability is an issue.

8.1 Handling Files

This section treats listing Application and Data Files, deleting and renaming Files, ensuring that all Files are Closed and verifying the presence of a given File.

Zortech C provides findfirst() and findnext() in library "dos" to access the current Directory for File entries. The Function findfirst(path, attr) takes two Arguments. The first Argument path is a String identifying the File or Files to DOS (possibly with wildcard Characters), e.g. "*.*". The second Argument is an Integer Mask of the required attribute bits, e.g. 0 for all "normal" Files, 0xFF for all Files. The Function findnext() takes no Arguments. Both return a Pointer to struct FIND, the first (or next) Directory entry satisfying path and attr. The Function findfirst() returns Pointer NULL if no such File is found. This property is used in 8.1.7. to verify the presence of a given File.

8.1.1 Display a list of Applications
```
system("dir *.c");
```
or:
```
system("dir *.exe");
```

8.1.2 Display a list of all Files in the current Directory
```
system("dir");
```

8.1.3 Display a list of data Files with given extension *.TXT
```
system("dir *.txt");
```

8.1.4 Close all Files currently Open

Files must be closed individually. See 12.2.5. All open files are closed by normal termination, also by

```
exit(0);
```

8.1.5 Rename a data File

```
#include <stdio.h>
...
rename("myold.dat","mynew.dat");
```

8.1.6 Delete an unwanted data File FRED.TXT

```
#include <io.h>
...
unlink("fred.txt");
```

8.1.7 Verify the presence of data File FRED.TXT

```
#include <dos.h>
...
if ( findfirst("fred.txt",0xFF) ) {...}
```

Executes {...} if **FRED.TXT** is present.

WARNING: Compile with the flag: −a so as to suppress alignment in Structure definitions.
or:

```
#include <dos.h>
struct FIND *p;
...
if ( (p=findfirst("fred.txt",0xFF))!=NULL ) {...}
```

Executes {...} if **FRED.TXT** is present. The Phrase: !=NULL is redundant, but avoids a Compiler warning message. struct FIND is defined in <dos.h> and is the Type returned by findfirst(), findnext().

Pointing p at this returned Value allows data concerning the File to be accessed using such constructs as:

```
p->attribute, p->time, p->date, p->size, p->name.
```

8.2 Handling Drives and Directories

Although system() might be used for the purpose, Zortech C provides mkdir(path), chdir(path) and rmdir(path) in the library "direct" to make, change-to and remove a Directory. The String Argument path is the required Directory pathname.

8.2.1 Change the current Drive to A:

```
system("a:");
```

8.2.2 Change the current Directory to C:\BATCH\FILES
```
chdir("c:\batch\files");
```

8.2.3 Create a new Directory, NEWDIR
```
mkdir("newdir");
```
returns 0 if created OK, -1 otherwise.
`"newdir"` may be replaced by any valid pathname.

8.3 Handling DOS

This is done, as 8.0 explains, with the Function: `system()`. If `system()` is called with an empty or void Argument, DOS runs interactively (see 8.3.2). Note that `system()` runs a fresh version of the DOS Command processor COMMAND.COM. When this terminates it takes its environment with it and any changed environment strings altered using `SET` will revert back to what they were before the `system()` call. If desired to access an environment string, e.g. `PATH`:
```
char *s; …; s = getenv("PATH");
```

8.3.1 Cause DOS to Execute a String containing VER as a Command
```
system("ver");
```

8.3.2 Enter DOS in its conversational mode
```
system("command");
```

8.3.3 Quit DOS and resume Execution of Application
```
C>exit
```

9

Hardware Devices: find status and control them

Zortech C provides relatively low-level support for interfacing with the PC Hardware. This chapter treats the available support for audible signals, the microprocessor's own I/O ports, the parallel Port (DOS standard device PRN) which usually serves a Line Printer, Screen control for text only (graphics are treated in chapter 5) and the System Clock/Calendar, accessed though the ANSI standard library "time".

9.1 Audible signals

Zortech C provides inconvenient support for the C3S tasks which require both pitch and duration to be specified (see 9.1.1). The Function sound_beep() takes one Integer Argument, pitch. The Function sound-tone() is the most flexible but requires experimentation to use effectively. The first Argument specifies duration in terms of the number of cycles to emit, Arguments 2 and 3 specify duration of "high" and "low" respectively to the sound device, which together determine wavelength (and timbre to some extent). We offer in 9.1.4 code for the Function soundtone() which takes Arguments pitch (in Hertz) and duration (in secs).

9.1.1 What facilities relate to sound production?
```
sound_tone() sound_beep() sound_click()
```
These are defined in: <sound.h>

9.1.2 Ring the Bell once
```
sound_beep(1331);
```
or:
```
putchar(7);
```

9.1.3 Emit "cuckoo" (E, C, with slight pause between)
```
soundnote(330,.2); silence(.02);
  soundnote(262,.2);
```
For definitions of soundnote(), silence(), see 9.1.4.

9.1.4 Emit middle-C with 1-second duration
```
#define REFERENCE 1190000L /* adjust for CPU
  speed */
#define ONESECOND 20000L /* adjust for CPU speed
  */
soundnote(unsigned,double); silence(double); /*
  fwd refs */
...
soundnote(262,1.0);
...
soundnote(pitch,duration)
unsigned pitch; double duration;
{
 unsigned saved, j;
 outp(67,182); /* i/o mode */
 j = (unsigned) (REFERENCE/pitch);
 outp(66, j); outp(66, j>>8);
 saved = inp(97); outp(97,79); /* start sounding
  */
```

```
  silence(duration); /* used as pause */
  outp(97,saved); /* stop sound */
}
silence(duration)
double duration;
{
  long i, j;
  j = (long) (duration*ONESECOND);
  for (i=0; i<j; i++) /* do nothing */;
}
```

9.1.5 Play a scale legato, tempo moderato, ending with middle-C

```
int note[] = {131,147,165,175,196,220,247,262};
...
for (i=0; i<8; i++) {
  soundnote(note[i], 0.2);
  silence(0.05);
}
```

For definitions of soundnote(), silence(), see 9.1.4.

9.1.6 Alter the timbre of the notes played

```
void sound_tone(int cycles, int uptime, int dntime);
/* above is as already declared in <sound.h> */
...
sound_tone(1000, 100, 100);
sound_tone(1000, 150, 50);
sound_tone(1000, 190, 10);
sound_tone(1000, 199, 1);
```

Experiment with different values of uptime, dntime.
All give the same frequency determined by (uptime+dntime), with
duration determined by: cycles.

9.2 Input/Output Ports

These Ports are those seen by the (8086/8) microprocessor and accessed
by the IN and OUT machine instructions. See 9.1.4 for a sample usage.

9.2.1 Read Byte from the Port Address N

```
unsigned z; ...; z = inp(N);
```

9.2.2 Write Byte to the Port Address N

```
unsigned z; ...; outp(N,z);
```

9.3 Line Printer (device: PRN)

Zortech C offers no specialised support for controlling the Line Printer directly from the Program. The C3S tasks of page width, page-feed, line-feed and printing a line of text are performed here by invoking DOS services via `system()` or the general-purpose I/O Functions `write()`, `putc()` and `fputs()`.

9.3.1 Set line width to 80 columns
```
system("mode prn: 80");
```

9.3.2 Set line width to 132 columns
```
system("mode prn: 132");
```

9.3.3 Eject the current page
```
write(4,"\014",1);
```
or:
```
putc(12, stdprn);
```

9.3.4 Print a blank line
```
write(4,"\n",1);
```
or:
```
putc(10, stdprn);
```

9.3.5 Output a line: ITEMS OUTSTANDING to both Screen and Line Printer
```
#include <string.h>
char msg[] = "ITEMS OUTSTANDING\n";
...
write(1,msg,strlen(msg));
write(4,msg,strlen(msg));
```
Five standard devices are always open: 0=Keyboard, 1=Screen, 2=Error (usually Screen), 3=Auxiliary, 4=Line Printer.
or:
```
#include <stdio.h>
#include <string.h>
char msg[] = "ITEMS OUTSTANDING\n";
...
fputs(msg,stdout); fputs(msg,stdprn);
```
Five standard streams are always open: `stdin`=Keyboard, `stdout`=Screen, `stderr`=Error (usually Screen), `stdaux`=Auxiliary, `stdprn`=Line Printer.

9.3.6 Print a line: ITEMS OUTSTANDING without typing it on the Screen
```
write(4,"ITEMS OUTSTANDING\n",strlen(msg));
```

or:
```
fputs("ITEMS OUTSTANDING\n",stdprn);
```

9.4 Screen control

This section treats the problem of clearing parts of the Screen and positioning text precisely by prior placement of the Cursor. This can entail finding out the current Cursor position first.

For complete hardware-independence at the expense of speed, use printf() to send the ANSI standard Escape sequences to the Screen. These require the line:
```
DEVICE = ANSI.SYS
```
to appear in the DOS system file CONFIG.SYS. 9.4.1 shows a sample of their use. For the full list of ANSI Escape sequences consult the DOS Operating System Reference Manual.

In place of ANSI Escape sequences, the specialised support for fast PC Screen control provided by Zortech is used after 9.4.1. This is a package of Functions in library "disp" all having Names beginning with: disp_... For the proper usage of these Functions see 9.4.1.

9.4.1 Clear the Screen
```
#include <stdio.h>
...
printf("\x1b[2J"); /* ANSI Escape Sequence:
    {Esc}[2J */
```
or:
```
#include <stdlib.h>
...
system("cls");
```
or:
```
#include <disp.h>
...
disp_open(); /* must precede all disp_ calls */
...
disp_move(0,0); disp_eeop();
...
disp_close();
```

9.4.2 Clear the current Screen line
```
disp_move(disp_cursorrow,0); disp_eeol();
```

9.4.3 Clear the current Screen line to the right of the Cursor position
```
disp_eeol();
```

9.4.4 Place Cursor in top left hand corner of Screen
```
disp_move(0,0);
```

9.4.5 Place Cursor in row I, column J of Screen
```
disp_move(i,j);
```

9.4.6 Make Variable I the current Cursor row
```
i = disp_cursorrow;
```
disp_cursorrow must be treated as read-only.

9.4.7 Make Variable J the current Cursor column
```
j = disp_cursorcol;
```
disp_cursorcol must be treated as read-only.

9.4.8 Move Cursor (non-destructively) N positions right
```
disp_move(disp_cursorrow,disp_cursorcol+N);
```

9.4.9 Move Cursor (non-destructively) N positions left
```
disp_move(disp_cursorrow,disp_cursorcol-N);
```

9.4.10 Move Cursor (non-destructively) N rows down
```
disp_move(disp_cursorrow+N,disp_cursorcol);
```

9.4.11 Move Cursor (non-destructively) N rows up
```
disp_move(disp_cursorrow-N,disp_cursorcol);
```

9.4.12 Print Variable N at upper left of Screen, then restore existing Cursor position
```
int row, col;
...
row = disp_cursorrow; col = disp_cursorcol;
disp_move(0,0);
disp_printf("%d",n);
disp_move(row,col);
```

9.4.13 Print two Asterisks with N Spaces between them
```
putchar('*');
for (i=0; i<N; i++) putchar(' ');
putchar('*');
```

9.4.14 Generate M blank lines beneath current Cursor position
```
disp_move(disp_cursorrow,0);
for (i=0; i<M; i++) {
 disp_putc('\n');
 disp_eeol();
```

```
}
```

9.5 System Clock/Calendar

This section considers not only accessing the System Clock/Calendar to move date and time into Program Variables in a specified format, but also timing the interval between two Events (Keystrokes in this case) and pausing for a stated interval or until a stated time. C supports these tasks by means of the ANSI standard library "time". This library does not support alteration of the System Clock/Calendar, so instead we employ system() to issue DOS DATE and TIME Commands to do this.

The samples need the preceding lines (as appropriate):
```
#include <time.t>
#include <string.t>
#include <stdio.h>
```

9.5.1 Make Variable Z the current date in System-defined format
```
char z[25]; /* ...or longer */
time_t t;
...
t = time(NULL); /* No. of secs since the year dot
    */
strcpy(z, ctime(&t)); /* make a legible timestamp
    */
z[24] = '\0'; /* remove final '\n' */
strcpy(z+10, z+19); /* remove time-of-day */
```

Zortech C yields z in the form:
```
Mon Nov 27 10:33:00 1989
```

which we next convert to:
```
Mon Nov 27 1989
```

9.5.2 Make Variable Z the current date as a String in UK format: 29-11-90
```
time_t t; struct tm *tp;
int d,m,y; char z[10];
...
t = time(NULL); tp = localtime(&t);
d = tp->tm_mday;
m = tp->tm_mon;
y = tp->tm_year;
sprintf(z,"%2d-%2d-%2d",d,m,y);
```

Note that struct tm is declared in <time.h> to be:

```
struct tm { int
tm_sec, tm_min, tm_hour,
tm_mday, tm_mon, tm_year,
tm_wday, /*weekday*/
tm_yday, /*day-of-year*/
tm_isdst /*daylight-saving-time indicator*/ };
```

9.5.3 Make Variable Z the current date in USA format: 11-29-90

as 9.5.2, but with:
```
sprintf(z,"%2d-%2d-%2d",m,d,y);
```

9.5.4 Make Variable Z the time-of-day as a String in System-defined format

```
char z[8]; time_t t;
...
t = time(NULL);
strncpy(z, ctime(&t)+11, 8); z[8] = '\0';
```

Zortech C yields z in the form:
```
15:45:00
```

9.5.5 Make Variable Z the time-of-day as a String: 15:45

```
char z[5]; time_t t;
...
t = time(NULL);
strncpy(z, ctime(&t)+11, 5); z[5] = '\0';
```

For explanation see 9.5.4.

9.5.6 Alter the current date to 1st March, 1990

```
system("date 01/03/90");
```

Note that whether this should be 01/03/90 or 03/01/90 is a DOS dependency. Day-before-Month pertains if the DOS system file CONFIG.SYS contains the line:
```
COUNTRY=044
```

9.5.7 Alter the current date to 1st March, 2001

```
system("date 01/03/2001");
```

9.5.8 Alter the time-of-day to 3.45 pm

```
system("time 15:45");
```

9.5.9 Wait for the next Keystroke, make Z the waiting duration in seconds

```
time_t t, tt; double z;
```

```
...
time(&t); getch(); time(&tt);
z = difftime(t,tt);
```

9.5.10 Suspend Execution for N seconds (approximately)
```
sleep ((time_t) N);
/*...resume*/
```

9.5.11 Suspend Execution for one-tenth of a second
On some PC Compatibles the timing Functions do not resolve intervals
to less than 1 sec. Thus the technique of 9.5.10 will not necessarily
work. Hence adapt `silence()` as defined in 9.1.4.

9.5.12 Suspend Execution until 4.30 pm
```
time_t t; struct tm *tp;
int hour, min;
...
hour = min = 0;
while ((hour!=16)||(min!=30)) {
  t = time(NULL); tp = localtime(&t);
  hour = tp->tm_hour; min = tp->tm_min;
  sleep(1); /*optional*/
  }
/*...resume*/
```

10

Keyboard: inputting data and recognising Keystrokes

This chapter considers in 10.1 the (prompted) inputting of various kinds
of numeral and the range of what is valid. In 10.2 techniques for
accepting a string or a line of input are treated, typically yes/no or a
numeral. Then in 10.3 - 10.6 the problems of responding to single
Keystrokes are addressed.

A Program may need to prompt the user for a number, or a series of
numbers, or a string of text, the result to be placed in some Variable.
Most Languages explicitly support the input of a number to a Numeric
Variable. However how this facility behaves when the user does not
type-in a number of the correct form may not be what you want. For

instance, the Program may halt with an Error. You may therefore wish to accept input as a String and convert the Numerals it contains by the techniques of 3.5.

10.1 Accept a Number from the Keyboard

C offers a variety of support facilities for inputting numbers, but here we mainly offer `scanf()`, the most powerful. The Function `scanf()` resembles `printf()` in reverse (although not entirely), being controlled by a comparable format String which is provided as Argument 1. See Chapter 4 for sample usage of `printf()` and Appendix D for a comparative summary of `printf()` and `scanf()` conventions regarding the format String.

The Function `scanf()` returns an Integer, the number of conversions successfully undertaken. The input stream must match the format String for all conversions to be completed. Note that a single Space in the format String however will match one or more Spaces in the input stream.

10.1.1 Accept a sequence of Digits terminated by Carriage Return, setting Numeric Variable Z to its Value
```
int z; ...; scanf("%d",&z);
```
or:
```
float z; ...; scanf("%e",&z);
```
or:
```
float z; ...; scanf("%f",&z);
```
or:
```
double z; ...; scanf("%le",&z);
```
or:
```
double z; ...; scanf("%lf",&z);
```
See 10.1.8 for effect of using `"%e"` rather than `"%f"`.
See Appendix D for a table of %-codes.

10.1.2 What is the Prompt issued by this Statement at Runtime?
None. Cursor waits at current Screen position.

10.1.3 Make the Prompt become TYPE A NUMBER--
```
puts("TYPE A NUMBER--"); scanf("%d",&z);
```

10.1.4 What are the restrictions on the choice of Variable Z?
Must be of appropriate Type to match the %-code, viz:
```
(int)    for "%d"
(float)  for "%e" and "%f"
(double) for "%le" and "%lf".
```

10.1.5 What happens if a non-valid Number is typed-in?

Digits are converted until the first Separator/Terminator (Space, Tab or Carriage Return) or the first non-matching Character. If there are no valid Digits then z becomes 0.

Non-matching Characters force an EOF Condition and are left on the input stream (viz. stdin in this case). These will corrupt successive scanf(...) Statements unless they are first removed, e.g. by following scanf() by:

```
fflush(stdin);
```

10.1.6 Is this valid? 32768

Yes, but "%d" yields z==(-32768).

10.1.7 Is this valid? 999999999999999

Yes, but "%d" yields z==32767.

10.1.8 Is this valid? 1.2345E-15

Yes, but for "%e" (and its variants) only. "%f" will match only the 1.2345 part.

10.1.9 Is this valid? Null

No. Program expects further (non-Blank) input.

10.1.10 Is this valid? 12 secs

In theory, yes. Treated as 12.
But see 10.1.5.

10.1.11 Is this valid? 12 34

No. Treated as 12. See 10.1.5.

10.1.12 Is this valid? 1,023.45

No. Treated as 1. All Numeric "%"-codes stop matching at the Comma. See 10.1.5.

10.1.13 Is this valid? X+1

No. Treated as 0. See 10.1.5.

10.1.14 Accept two Numbers on the same line, placing them in X and Y.

```
float x,y; ...; scanf("%e %e",&x,&y);
```

10.1.15 How may the Numbers be separated?

By one or more "white space" Characters, viz. Space, Tab or Carriage Return.

10.1.16 What happens if only one Number is typed-in?

Carriage Return is treated as "white space", see 10.1.15. Program therefore expects further (non-Blank) input, in order to match the second `"%d"`.

10.1.17 What happens if more than two Numbers are typed-in?
Subsequent Numbers remain in the input stream (`stdin`).

10.2 Accept a sequence of Characters from the Keyboard

This section is primarily concerned with accepting raw text in place of more restricted data, like Numerals and yes/no answers, in order to analyse free-form replies and patch-up users' mistakes.

10.2.1 Accept a sequence of Characters terminated by Carriage Return into a String Variable Z
```
char *z; ...; gets(z);
```

10.2.2 Is the terminating Carriage Return included at the end of Z?
No. A terminating Null (`'\0'`) is appended instead.

10.2.3 Accept a valid Numeral as a String and convert to the corresponding Number N
```
char *z; int n; ...; gets(z); sscanf(z,"%d",&n);
```
Adapt 10.1.1 for inputting to other Numeric Types.

10.2.4 Is abc converted to ABC automatically on input?
No.

10.2.5 Accept a free-format yes/no answer terminated by Carriage Return, print ANSWER IS NO if there is a leading n or N
```
char *z; ...; scanf("%s",z);
if (tolower(*z)=='n') printf("\nANSWER IS NO");
```

10.3 Wait for a Character Key to be struck before resuming Execution

You may wish your Program to pause to let the user read the Screen, resuming when a given Key (or any Character Key) is struck. Alternatively you may wish to accept a user option as a single Keystroke, e.g. Y/N, or a Letter or Digit.

10.3.1 Wait for any Character Key to be struck
```
getch();
```

or:
```
(void) getch();
```
The (void) is redundant, but serves to indicate that the returned value is discarded.

or:
```
#include <conio.h>
...
while ( !kbhit() );
```
Note that after kbhit() the Character which has been hit remains in the input stream (stdin) to be read by a subsequent getch(), scanf(...), etc.

10.3.2 Wait for a Keystroke, accepting Carriage Return only
```
while( getch() !='\r');
```

10.3.3 Wait for a single Keystroke, accepting Space only
```
while( getch() !=' ');
```

10.3.4 Wait for a single Keystroke, inviting Keys y, Y, n or N, then print NO if n or N, otherwise print YES
```
int z;
...
z = tolower(getch());
if (z=='n') puts("NO"); else puts("YES");
```

10.4 Detect a Keystroke, then determine which Key has been struck

Some Programs which respond to single Keystrokes cannot wait for a Keystroke to occur, but must continue processing, e.g. reading a Port or the System Clock, or updating a real-time display. Whereas getch() will take the next Character out of the Keyboard Buffer, if this is empty the System will enter the wait state. Zortech C provides the Function kbhit() to test whether the Keyboard Buffer is empty or not before Executing getch(). Note also the Function bioskey() for the most general examination of the Keyboard.

This section also considers the contents of the Keyboard Buffer, as returned by getch(), resulting from the various non-Character or non-printable Keys, including selected {Ctl-} and {Alt-} combinations.

10.4.1 Make Variable Z the next Keystroke waiting in the Keyboard Buffer, continue if Buffer empty
```
unsigned char z;
...
if (kbhit()) z = getch();
```

10.4.2 What does Z become if the Keyboard Buffer is empty?
z is unchanged.

10.4.3 Does Z contain the ASCII code of the Key?
Yes.

10.4.4 What does Z become after non-ASCII key?
Zero if the Key has an Extended Keycode.
To fetch the Extended Keycode, which follows the Null Character in the input stream:
```
if (z=='\0') z = getch();
```

10.4.5 What does Z become after {Esc}?
27

10.4.6 What does Z become after Function Key {f1}, ... {f10}?
(Extended) 59, 60, ... 68 (See 10.4.4).

10.4.7 What does Z become after {Backspace}, {Enter}, {Return}, {Tab}?
8, 13, 13, 9

10.4.8 What does Z become after {Up}, {Down}, {Left}, {Right}?
(Extended) 72, 80, 75, 77 (See 10.4.4).

10.4.9 What does Z become after {PgUp}, {PgDn}, {Home}, {End}?
(Extended) 73, 81, 71, 79 (See 10.4.4).

10.4.10 What does Z become after {Ctl-A}, {Ctl-B}, ... {Ctl-Z}?
1, 2, ..., 26
Note that {Ctl-Z} will subsequently halt the Program.

10.4.11 What does Z become after {Alt-1}, {Alt-2}, ... {Alt-9}, {Alt-0}?
(Extended) 120, 121, ..., 128, 129.

10.5 Recognise the striking of a Function Key or {Esc}

10.5.1 Execute a given Statement whenever {f1} is struck
Not directly supported in Zortech C. Must adapt the technique of 10.4.

10.5.2 Execute a given Statement whenever {Esc} is struck
Not directly supported in Zortech C. Must adapt the technique of 10.4.

10.6 Recognise the striking of a given {Ctl-} or {Alt-} combination

Zortech C does not support the task of writing an Event-driven Program which will Execute given Statements whenever a given Key or Key-combination is struck. Instead the techniques of 10.4 must be employed to inspect the Keyboard Buffer periodically.

One exception is {Ctl-Break}. This is normally trapped by DOS and leads to the Program being instantly terminated, possibly leaving Files Open. Zortech C furnishes support for intercepting {Ctl-Break} and resuming the Run after Executing given Statements.

10.6.1 Execute a given Statement whenever {Ctl-A} ... etc. is struck

Not directly supported in Zortech C. Must adapt the technique of 10.4.

10.6.2 Disable/enable the DOS interrupt action of {Ctl-Break}

See 10.6.3.

10.6.3 Execute a given Statement whenever {Ctl-Break} is struck

```
#include <int.h>
#define STACKSIZE 256 /*the minimum allowed*/
#define VECTOR 0x23 /*DOS interrupt*/
volatile int cc;
int ctlbreak(); /*declared to serve as argument*/
...
int_intercept(VECTOR,ctlbreak,STACKSIZE);
...
int_restore(VECTOR);
...
int ctlbreak()
{
  cc = 0; /*Statement to be executed*/
  return 1;
}
```

Considerable restrictions apply to the Statements of ctlbreak(). These include:

(1) No I/O, DOS, BIOS or non-re-entrant Function calls.
(2) Declare any Variables assigned (e.g. cc) as: volatile.

See Zortech C Interrupt Package documentation.

10.6.4 Execute a given Statement whenever {Alt-1}, {Alt-2}, ... {Alt-9}, {Alt-0} is struck

Not directly supported in Zortech C. Must adapt the technique of 10.4.

11

Main Memory: control allocation and placement within it

C generally looks after the allocation and release of Memory for Program code and Variables without the programmer needing to be aware in detail how this is done. However there are circumstances when you might wish to take control of these activities yourself.

11.1 Memory space

11.1.1 Make Z the amount of free space in Bytes

Not directly supported in C.

Use `malloc()` to attempt to allocate space and check for the returned Pointer Value `NULL`.

11.1.2 Release unwanted Memory space
```
free(p)
```

p must be a Pointer Value returned by `malloc()`, `calloc()` or `realloc()`.

11.2 Obtaining Memory space

11.2.1 Reserve 16K of Memory for resident machine code
See 11.2.2.

11.2.2 Allocate a block of 16K Bytes, setting Variable A to point to the first Byte
```
char *a; ...; a = malloc(16384);
```

11.3 Layout of items in Memory

Normally you will only want to alter the Value of a Variable by regular means, e.g. Assignment, which the System undertakes correctly without you having to know the layout in Memory of that Value. However on occasions the Bytes or the Bit Pattern of a given Variable need to be located in Memory and possibly altered. This section considers how to find the Address of the starting Byte of the Value of z, the Type of z and the Bit Pattern of its Value if an Integer.

C provides very good support for these tasks by means of Pointer constructs, one of the strongest features of the Language.

11.3.1 What sort of Address is used as a Pointer Value?

Two sorts of Pointer Value are used:

(1) the "far" Pointer (4 Byte) for an Address anywhere in Memory,

(2) the "near" Pointer (2 Byte) for an Address within the same Segment. This Pointer Value consists of the Offset only.

Pointers can be explicitly declared far or near. The default sort of Pointer is determined by the choice of "memory model", selected by means of a "switch" or Argument when calling the Compiler:

```
-mS "small model": code<64K, data<64K
-mM "medium model": code<1M, data<64K
-mC "compact model": code<64K, data<1M
-mL "large model": code<1M, data<1M
```

There is also a "tiny model": code+data<64K, a special case of the "small model". Using -mT will automatically select the "tiny model" and generate a .COM File instead of an .EXE File. See 1.3.13.

11.3.2 Make A the Address of the starting Byte of the data in Variable Z

```
char *a; ...; a = (char *) &z;
```
or:
```
void *a; ...; a = &z;
```
Note that these assume z is not a String Variable, e.g. it is Numeric. If z is a String Variable then it has the Type of a Pointer already, and the preceding Ampersand (&) must be omitted, e.g.
```
char z[80]; void *a; ...; a = z;
```

11.3.3 Make Y the Type (Integer, String, etc.) of the Variable Z

Not directly supported in C. However the following provides the number of Bytes allocated to the given Variable z, which is indicative of its type:
```
y = sizeof z;
```

11.3.4 Make Z the Value of the Byte at address, A

```
unsigned char z; ...; z = (unsigned char) *a;
```
assuming a is as in 11.3.2.

71

11.3.5 Alter the first two Characters of the String Variable S to Asterisk (ASCII 42)

```
char *s; ...; *s = *(s+1) = 42;
```
or:
```
char *s,*p; ...; p = s; *p = *p++ = '*';
```

11.3.6 Alter the last Character of the String Variable S to Asterisk (ASCII 42)

The last Character is the one before the terminating ' \0' .
```
char *s; ...; *(s + strlen(s) - 1) = 42;
```

11.3.7 Make String S the Bit Pattern of an Integer Value N

```
char s[2]; int n;
...
*(int *)s = n;
```
Note that in Zortech C 2-Byte Integers are stored in low/high order. The above preserves the same order in s . The following however reverses the Byte order:
```
s[1] = *(char *)&n; s[0] = *((char *)&n+1);
```

11.3.8 Make Variable N the Integer Value of a 16 Bit Pattern held in String S

```
n = *(int *)s;
```
Note that in Zortech C 2-Byte Integers are stored in low/high order. The above preserves the same order as in s . The following however reverses the Byte order:
```
n = ((unsigned)s[1]) + (256*(unsigned)s[0]);
```

11.4 Contents of individual Bytes in Memory

This section treats retrieving and altering the contents of the Byte at a given Address, including individual Bits within that Byte. See the remarks at 11.3 concerning the need (if ever) to do this.

Note that the C3S tasks refer to Address A. The examples assume that you have set a Pointer Variable a to point to some required target. C discourages specifying an Address as a Numeric Constant. If however you do need to do this, then Zortech C provides built-in Functions peek() and poke() to access a segment/offset Address. Their Function prototypes are:
```
void peek(unsigned seg, unsigned offset, void
  *buf, int numbytes);
void poke(unsigned seg, unsigned offset, void
  *buf, int numbytes);
```

11.4.1 Make Integer Z the Value of the Byte at Address A
```
int z; char *a; ...; z = (int) *a;
```

11.4.2 Make Integer Z the Value of the double-Byte at Address A
```
int z; char *a; ...; z = *(int *) a;
```
Note that double-Bytes are interpreted as Integers in low/high order.

11.4.3 Change the Value of the Byte at Address A to Hex: 2A
```
*a = 0x2a;
```

11.4.4 Change the Value of the Byte at Address A to the ASCII code of Asterisk (*)
```
*a = '*';
```

11.4.5 Change the Value of the Byte at Address A to Integer Value N
```
*a = N;
```

11.4.6 What if N is Negative?
Excess high-order Bits are dropped. Thus `(N==-1)` would give `((*a)==0xff)`

11.4.7 What if N>255, e.g. N = Hex: 789A?
Excess high-order Bits are dropped to give `((*a)==0x9a)`

11.4.8 Set Bit 0 of the Byte at Address A to 1
```
*a = (*a) & 0x80;
```
Note: Mask `0x80` is `1000 0000`

11.4.9 Set Bit 0 of the Byte at Address A to 0
```
*a = (*a) | 0x7f;
```
Note: Mask `0x7F` is `0111 1111`

12

Move Data between a named File and a set of Variables

This chapter considers writing the data in Program Variables to disk as a File and reading it back again into Variables. A File may be Opened for reading, writing (afresh) or updating. Opened Files must be Closed after use, collections of Variables, or entire Structures, may be written to the File in successive chunks (Records) and read back again.

Also considered are the problems of writing Numeric Variables to disk as legible Numerals rather than as Bit patterns, and of moving the File Record Pointer, which determines at which Byte of the File the next retrieval commences.

12.1 Can a single Record consist of:

12.1.1 More than one Value?
Yes.

12.1.2 Both Integers and Strings?
Yes.

12.1.3 A varying number of Values?
Yes, but inputting and outputting the correct number of Values must be explicitly handled by the programmer.

12.1.4 A Structure?
Yes.

12.2 Open and close a sequential File
There are two families of Functions, low-level `<dos.h>` and high-level `<stdio.h>`. They are not intended to be mixed. In what follows the high-level solution is given first, then the low-level one. Assume throughout:

```
#include <stdio.h>
```

for the high-level solutions, and:

```
#include <dos.h>
```

for the low-level solutions.

The low-level Functions are mainly implemented by direct calls to DOS. Each open File is allocated an Integer called the File Descriptor. The Variable: fd, of Type (int), will be used below to hold this Value. For portability, use only high-level Functions. With these Functions each open File is a "stream", represented by a File Pointer. The Variable: f, of Type (FILE *), will be used below to hold this Value.

12.2.1 Open for reading data into Memory from a File named MYFILE.DAT

```
#include <stdio.h>
...
FILE *f;
...
f = fopen("myfile.dat","r");
```

Note: mode "r" opens the File in text mode. Appending "b" to the Value of mode (e.g. to give "rb") opens the File in binary mode. As a result, no translations are performed. See notes at 12.3.17.

```
#include <dos.h>
#include <io.h>
...
int fd;
...
fd = open("myfile.dat",O_RDONLY);
```

O_RDONLY, O_WRONLY, O_RDWR are #defined in <dos.h> to be 0, 1 and 2 respectively.

12.2.2 Open for writing out a fresh File named MYFILE.DAT to the Diskette

```
#include <stdio.h>
...
FILE *f;
...
f = fopen("myfile.dat","w");
```

See 12.2.1 for text mode versus binary mode.

```
#include <dos.h>
#include <io.h>
...
int fd;
...
fd = open("myfile.dat",O_WRONLY);
```

See 12.2.1 for O_WRONLY.

12.2.3 Open for updating an existing File named MYFILE.DAT

```
#include <stdio.h>
...
FILE *f;
...
f = fopen("myfile.dat","a");
```
As well as "a", can have modes "r+", "w+" (for both reading and writing) and "a+" (for both appending and writing).
See 12.2.1 for text mode versus binary mode.

```
#include <dos.h>
#include <io.h>
...
int fd;
...
fd = open("myfile.dat",O_RDWR);
```
See 12.2.1 for O_RDWR.

12.2.4 How many Files can be Open at the same time?
Limited by available Memory space.

12.2.5 Close a given Open File
```
fclose(f);
```
or:
```
close(fd);
```

12.2.6 Close all Open Files
Not supported in C for unspecified Files.
Programmer must call `fclose()` for each File Opened by `fopen()` (or `close()` for each File Opened by `open()`).
All Files are Closed automatically by normal Program termination or by `exit()`.

12.3 Write and read back formatted data
The standard Functions `fprintf()` and `fscanf()` in library "stdio" permit Numerals to be written to and read back from a File in the same format as `printf()` writes to the Screen and `scanf()` reads from the Keyboard. We consider the patterns of Bytes that result from writing several Numeric Variables at once, or one-at-a-time in a Loop, as well as mixed Strings and Numbers.

Note that the "natural" way of writing Numbers (see 12.3.2) does not necessarily result in a text File, i.e. with records terminating in Carriage Return + Newline and the File ending with EOF (ASCII 26) unless these Bytes are explicitly written, e.g. by means of Backslash (\) constructs (see Appendix B).

12.3.1 Iteratively write the Integers 101 to 105 to a new File MYFILE.DAT

```
FILE *f; int i;
...
f = fopen("myfile.dat","w");
for (i=101; i<=105; i++) fprintf(f," %d",i);
fclose(f);
```

12.3.2 What is the actual Character sequence of this File?

b101b102b103b104b105
where b=Space (ASCII 32).

12.3.3 Iteratively read back and type a series of Integers from the File MYFILE.DAT

```
int z; FILE *f;
...
f = fopen("myfile.dat","r");
while (fscanf(f,"%d",&z)!=EOF) printf(" %d",z);
fclose(f);
```

12.3.4 How does the treatment of Non-Integer Variables differ?

Declare z (float) instead of (int) and use "%f" instead of "%d".
or:
Declare z (double) instead of (int) and use "%lf" instead of "%d".

12.3.5 Write the Integers 101 to 105 to a new File MYFILE2.DAT as a single Record

```
FILE *f;
...
f = fopen("myfile2.dat","w");
fprintf(f," %d %d %d %d %d",101,102,103,104,105);
fclose(f);
```

12.3.6 What is the actual Character sequence of this File?

Same as 12.3.2. Some choice of Record Terminator can be used if desired, e.g. Newline. In that case "wb" is recommended. 12.3.5 would then become:

```
FILE *f;
...
f = fopen("myfile2.dat","wb");
fprintf(f,"%d%d%d%d%d\n",101,102,103,104,105);
fclose(f);
```

12.3.7 Read back the next five Integers from the File MYFILE2.DAT into the Variables U, V, W, X, Y

```
FILE *f; int u,v,w,x,y;
...
f = fopen("myfile2.dat","rb");
...
fscanf(f,"%d %d %d %d %d",&u,&v,&w,&x,&y);
```

Note that Space between "%d %d..." for fscanf() means that one or more Spaces will be matched. Final Space is not necessary.

12.3.8 Read back the next five Integers from the File MYFILE2.DAT into the first five elements of Array A

```
FILE *f; int a[5];
...
f = fopen("myfile2.dat","r");
...
for (i=0; i<5; i++) fscanf(f,"%d", &a[i]);
```

12.3.9 Write a new Integer 606 on the end of an existing File MYFILE.DAT

```
FILE *f;
...
f = fopen("myfile.dat","a");
fprintf(f," %d", 606);
```

12.3.10 Write String NOM, Integer AGE, Non-Integer HEIGHT on the end of an existing File MYFILE.DAT

```
FILE *f;
char nom[60]="Fred"; int age=21; float
  height=5.56;
...
f = fopen("myfile.dat","a");
fprintf(f," %s %d %f", nom,age,height);
```

12.3.11 Read back String NOM, Integer AGE, Non-Integer HEIGHT from the File MYFILE.DAT

```
FILE *f; char nom[60]; int age; float height;
...
f = fopen("myfile.dat","r");
...
fscanf(f," %s %d %f", nom, &age, &height);
```

Note that for this to work, the NOM Field is assumed not to contain Space(s). If NOM can contain Space, then choose a Character which cannot appear in NOM, e.g. Semicolon, and use %[^;] instead of %s to match any Character EXCEPT Semicolon. Then follow %[...] with literal Semicolon to match a Semicolon in the stream used to terminate NOM, e.g.

```
fscanf(f," %[^;];%d %f", nom, &age, &height);
```

12.3.12 What signals the end of a String?
Space, Carriage Return, Tab or Newline, if the "%s" conversion specification is used.
or:
Any specified Character(s) or Newline, if the "%[^...]" conversion specification is used.

12.3.13 What signals the end of a Record?
Whatever constitutes a Record is under the control of the Programmer, who must synchronise the stream with the format String.

12.3.14 Read the next J bytes from the File MYFILE.DAT into String Variable Z

```
FILE *f; char *z;
...
f = fopen("myfile.dat","rb");
fgets(z, J+1, f);
```

12.3.15 Will a particular Character stop a String being read?
Yes. Newline ('\n').

12.3.16 Step through the entire File MYFILE.DAT, moving each Record into Variable Z as a String

```
FILE *f; char z[60];
...
f = fopen("myfile.dat","rb");
while (fgets(z,N+1,f)!=NULL) {...}
```
Assumes N is maximum Record length.

12.3.17 Step through the entire File MYFILE.DAT Byte by Byte, typing each Character on the Screen

```
char z; FILE *f;
...
f = fopen("myfile.dat","rb");
while ((z=fgetc(f))!=EOF) putchar(z);
fclose(f);
```
Note that further Statements would be required to handle non-printing Characters moved into z.

WARNING: fgetc(f) and its cousins convert Carriage Return + Linefeed pairs ('\r\n') as found in DOS text Files to simple Linefeeds ('\n'), unless the File is opened in "binary mode" (i.e. "rb" instead of "r").

```
FILE *f;
unsigned char z, eof = EOF;
...
f = fopen("myfile.dat","r");
while ((z=fgetc(f))!=eof) putchar(z);
fclose(f);
```

The Byte code Hex:80 (and above) would cause (int) z to become
Hex:FF80 (and above) instead of Hex:0080, due to the phenomenon of
sign-bit propagation in Zortech C. However declaring z to be
(unsigned) requires it to be compared with (unsigned) eof
(Hex:00FF) in place of EOF. Otherwise (z==EOF) would remain
forever False, because EOF (==-1) is here interpreted as Hex:FFFF.

12.4 Alter the File Record Pointer

Zortech C supports manipulating the File Record Pointer with the
Functions fseek() to move it and ftell() to determine where it
points to. The Function rewind() is also available, to reset the File
Record pointer to the start of the File.

Assume unless otherwise stated that File has been opened with:

```
f = fopen(filename, mode);
```

where mode is "rb", "wb", ..., etc., i.e. not text mode but binary
mode. Otherwise the real and apparent positions of the File Pointer may
differ, for the reason stated in 12.3.17.

12.4.1 Let Z become the number of Records in the File F

Record count (as such) is not supported in C. If Records are of uneven
length, terminated (say) by '\n', then Programmer must count Records
by adapting the technique of 12.3.16. If Records are all the same length,
then use a Byte count and divide by the Record length.
In what follows, counts of Bytes and not Records will be used.

```
long z; FILE *f; ...; z = filesize("myfile.dat");
```
but not once the File is Open. Then use fseek() and ftell(), e.g.
```
long z; FILE *f;
...
f = fopen("myfile.dat","rb");
fseek(f, 0L, SEEK_END); z = ftell(f);
fseek(f, 0L, SEEK_SET); /*restore to start of
    File*/
```
SEEK_SET, SEEK_CUR and SEEK_END are #defined as 0, 1 and
2 respectively, in <io.h>.

12.4.2 Let Z become the position of the File Pointer of File F
```
long z; FILE *f; ...; z = ftell(f);
```
Note: z is now the position as a Byte count.

12.4.3 Set File Pointer to point at the first Record of File F
```
FILE *f; ...; fseek(f, 0L, SEEK_SET);
```
Note: 0L is (long) Zero.

12.4.4 Set File Pointer to point at the Nth Record of File F
```
FILE *f; ...; fseek(f, NN, SEEK_SET);
```
See 12.4.1 for SEEK_SET.
NN, of Type (long), stands for the count in Bytes of the position of
the Nth Record from the start of the File.

12.4.5 Is the first Record denoted by N=0 or N=1?
N=0.

**12.4.6 Advance the File Pointer of File F to skip the next
Record**
```
FILE *f; ...; fseek(f, (long) R, SEEK_CUR);
```
See 12.4.1 for SEEK_CUR.
R stands for the Record length.

13

Refer to a Label, Variable or Function indirectly

This chapter considers the task of referring to a Label, a Variable or a
Function indirectly, that is, not by means of its Identifier being written
directly into the Statement concerned, but determining at Run-time
which of a selection of Labels (Variables, Functions) should serve as the
target of a given Branch (Assignment, Execution).

13.1 Rationale of the concept of Indirect Reference

Sometimes a Program must specify an operation on some data item or
the Execution of some Subroutine, but it is not known until Runtime

which data item or which Subroutine. Thus where an Identifier would normally be specified in the source code, some Languages allow an "indirect reference" instead. The actual Identifier to be employed at Runtime might be held in a String Variable, or the actual Variable to be employed might be pointed-to by a Pointer Variable. Sometimes it is possible to gather the candidate Identifiers into a list, from which the Nth member can be selected at Runtime. All three are techniques for avoiding a direct reference to an Identifier in the source code, and in a sense support the same programming task.

13.2 Collections of Statement Labels

13.2.1 Branch to the Nth of a list of Labels

```
switch(n) {
  case 0: ...; break;
  case 1: ...; break;
  case 2: ...; break;
  ...
  default: ...; break;
  }
```

The Statement Labelled: `default:` is optional.

The Statement `break;` is optional immediately before `}` but is recommended for convenience of source code maintenance and checking. Omitting `break;` elsewhere will permit Execution to run on into the next Labelled Statement.

Labels for `case` are different from Labels serving as targets for `goto`. The former are Constants, (int) or (char), e.g. MYCONST: 'A': 65: 'XY':

The latter are simply Identifiers declared as being Labels by being used as such. There is no clash with other Identifiers used for Variables, etc.

```
enum lablist {LAB0, LAB1, LAB2};
...
switch(n) {
  case LAB0: ...; break;
  case LAB1: ...; break;
  case LAB2: ...; break;
  }
```

In effect LAB0, LAB1, LAB2 behave like Integer Constants, 0, 1, 2, thus matching the Value of n.

Optionally n can be declared (int) or else as:

```
enum lablist n;
```

in which case any Integer Value assigned to n needs recasting to (enum lablist).

13.2.2 What happens if N is outside the range of the list?
No operation takes place unless `default:` has been specified.

13.3 Collections of Variables

C is a compiled Language in which the Names of Variables are not available to the object Program. Therefore it is hard to refer to a selection of Variables as the subject of an Assignment, unless the members of that set can be identified with the Terms of an Array or Structure (maybe of Pointers) and so Indexed.

13.3.1 Make Z the Value of the Nth of a list of Variables, A, B, C

```
z = (n==0) ? a : (n==1) ? b : (n==2) ? c : -1;
```
z becomes -1 if n is not 0, 1 or 2.
The above construct demands a default Value for z (viz. -1 here).
Or:
```
int a, b, c;
int *vp[] = {&a, &b, &c}; /* array of ptrs to
   a,b,c*/
...
z = *vp[n];
```
z gets a bad Value if n is not 0, 1 or 2.

13.3.2 Place the Value of Z into the Nth of a list of Variables, A, B, C

```
switch(n) {
  case 0: a=z; break;
  case 1: b=z; break;
  case 2: c=z; break;
  }
```
No Operation takes place if n is not 0, 1 or 2.
Or:
```
*vp[n] = z;
```
a, b, c, vp defined as in 13.3.1.
Memory gets corrupted if n is not 0, 1 or 2.

13.3.3 What happens if N is outside the range of the list?
See notes after each solution above.

13.3.4 Let Z become the Value of a Variable identified by literal name held in NOM
Need to anticipate all the Identifiers of Variables that can occur as contents of `nom`.
```
char nom[31];
...
```

```
z=(!strcmp(nom,"aaa"))?aaa
: (!strcmp(nom,"bbb"))?bbb
: (!strcmp(nom,"ccc"))?ccc
: -1;
```

The Preprocessor can be used to simplify this Statement, e.g. as follows:
```
#define CF(x)   (!strcmp(nom,#x))?x
...
z = CF(aaa) : CF(bbb) : CF(ccc) : -1;
```

13.3.5 Alter the Value of a Variable identified by literal name held in NOM

Adapt technique of 13.3.4, or else use:
```
char *nom;
...
   if (!strcmp(nom,"aaa")) aaa=z;
else if (!strcmp(nom,"bbb")) bbb=z;
else if (!strcmp(nom,"ccc")) ccc=z;
```

13.4 Collections of Subroutines

13.4.1 Execute the Nth of a list of Subroutines, SUB1, SUB2, SUB3

Adapt the technique of 13.2.1, or else define an Array of Pointers to the required Subroutines:
```
void sub1(int), sub2(int), sub3(int);
void (*subn[])(int) = {sub1, sub2, sub3};
...
(*subn[n])(99); /* Execute the nth Subroutine */
...
/* Subroutine definitions... */
void sub1(int j)
{...}
void sub2(int j)
{...}
void sub3(int j)
{...}
```

13.4.2 Pass the Identifier of a Subroutine S as an Argument to another Subroutine

See 14.4.6.

13.4.3 Execute a Subroutine identified by one of the literal names, SUB1, SUB2, SUB3, held in NOM

Adapt the technique of 13.3.5.

13.5 Pointers and Based Variables

A Variable z is "Based" on a Pointer p by persuading the System to identify the target of p as the Value of z .

13.5.1 Why Base a Variable upon a Pointer Value?

Binary data, particularly that read from disk, may consist of the untranslated Memory-image of various Types of data. Such Binary data can be reconstituted in principle by Basing a Variable of the required Type upon a Pointer to its start. In this way a Structure can be written unformatted to a File and read back again.

13.5.2 Make Variable P point to the Numeric Variable Z

```
void *p; int z;
...
p = &z;
```

In general declare *p to be the same type as z, or else cast &z to the (Pointer) Type of p, e.g.

```
int *p; unsigned z;
...
p = (int *) &z;
```

13.5.3 Make Variable P point to the first Term of the Numeric Array, A

```
void *p; int a[] = {111, 222, 333};
...
p = &a[0];
```

or:

```
p = a;
```

13.5.4 Make Variable P point to the first Byte of the String S

```
void *p; char *s; ...; p = s;
```

or:

```
void *p; char s[60]; ...; p = s;
```

13.5.5 Base the Numeric Variable Z upon Pointer Value P

```
void *p; int *z; ...; z = p;
```

Casting p as (int *) is necessary if p is declared to be some other Pointer Type than (void *) or (int *), e.g.

```
char *p; int *z; ...; z = (int *) p;
```

The same technique can be adapted to other Numeric Types besides (int).

13.5.6 Base the Numeric Array A upon Pointer Value P

```
void *p; int *a, z; ...; a = p;
a[1] = 99; z = a[2]; /* etc... */
```

Since `a[]` has no allocated Memory space of its own, it should be declared as shown, i.e. without `[...]`.

Casting `p` as `(int *)` is necessary if `p` is declared to be some other Pointer Type than `(void *)` or `(int *)`, e.g.

```
char *p; int *a, z; ...; a = (int *) p;
```

13.5.7 Base the String Variable S upon Pointer Value P

```
void *p; char *s; ...; s = p;
```

Casting `p` as `(char *)` is necessary if `p` is declared to be some other Pointer Type than `(void *)` or `(char *)`, e.g.

```
unsigned char *p; char *s; ...; s = (char *) p;
```

14

Subroutines, Functions and Macros

This chapter considers how C supports the C3S concepts of Subroutine, Function and Macro. See 14.1 for their rationale in general. Subroutines and Functions are essentially the same construct in C, and are differentiated only by usage. Macros resemble Subroutines/Functions Syntactically, to the extent that you may not be aware that a given library Function is actually implemented as a Macro.

14.1 Rationale of concepts and their implementation

14.1.1 The concept of Subroutine

Subroutines are like miniature Programs serving the Main Program. If the Language supports the Subroutine concept then it is possible to enter a given Block of Statements from anywhere in the Program (called the Point of Invocation) and return reliably to the same Point of Invocation, without needing to write a list of the various possible return Labels into the Subroutine itself.

Subroutines in C are fundamentally no different from Functions (see 14.1.2) except in the way they are invoked, especially as regards the treatment of their returned Value, if any. Both Subroutines and Functions are referred-to in C terminology as "functions".

14.1.2 The concept of Function

Many Languages have built-in primitives to compute common mathematical functions. In C, however, libraries of standard Functions take the place of built-in primitives to provide such familiar mathematical functions as `sin(x)` and `cos(x)`. These standard Functions are essentially no different from user-defined Functions, except that in most C systems they are pre-Compiled for efficiency.

The Function facility in C allows the Value of a user-defined Function to be computed within a Block of Statements `{ ... }`. This Block is then appended to a "function declaration" which declares a given Identifier to be a Function, just as a "variable declaration" declares a given Identifier to be a Variable. The Function is Invoked by using that Identifier (followed by a list of Parameters) as a term in an Expression, just as one would a Variable. When the Expression is Evaluated, the Block is Executed (once for each occurrence of the Identifier) and the returned Value is substituted back in place of the Identifier.

A Function in C may be permitted to change the Values of Variables in the calling Program by using Pointers to Values, instead of the Values themselves, in the Parameter list of its Invoking Expression.

The facility to return a computed Value need not be used, or the Value so returned may be discarded by the Invoking Expression, which may consist of nothing else but the Identifier and its Parameter list. Thus the Subroutine facility within C is merely a special case of the Function facility. See 14.1.1.

14.1.3 The concept of Macro

Many Languages allow one or more (complex) Statements to be substituted in the Main Program by (much simpler) parameterisable constructs, often resembling Function Invocations. Unlike a Function, a Macro specifies a purely textual substitution of one sequence of Characters in the Program for another, and for that reason is generally more flexible.

The Macro facility within C permits Identifiers to be defined which are systematically replaced throughout the text of the Program with a designated arbitrary sequence of Characters. Thus:

```
#define MYNUM 123.56
```

replaces MYNUM wherever it occurs with 123.56.

The `#define` construct also permits symbolic Parameters to be specified within the substitution text, which are themselves replaced by the corresponding Argument in the Macro call. Thus:

```
#define SINC(x) sin(x)/(x)
```

will replace (e.g.)
```
... SINC(a+b) ...
```
wherever it occurs in a Statement with:
```
... sin(a+b)/(a+b) ...
```
Thus it is possible to emulate a Function call by in-line substitution of an equivalent Expression.

14.2 The Body of a Subroutine

This section considers the scope and limitations of the Statements which go to make up the Body of a given Subroutine, and to what extent it behaves like an autonomous Program within a Program.

14.2.1 Invoke the Subroutine MYSUB within the Program
```
mysub();
```

14.2.2 Can MYSUB be invoked directly in the interactive session?
No. It must be called directly or indirectly using a Program Statement.

14.2.3 Branch from MYSUB back to the Point of Invocation
```
return;
```
Implicit `return` is performed upon normal exit from the outermost Block `{ ... }` of the Body of `mysub()`. Therefore an explicit `return` Statement is rarely needed, except to return a computed Value from a user-written Function. See 14.3.9, 14.5.4.

14.2.4 Branch from MYSUB to a labelled Statement in the Main Program
Not directly supported in C. Use `setjmp()` and `longjmp()` as defined in `<setjmp.h>`. The intention of this facility is to allow Error escapes from low-level Subroutines to share common Error-handling Statements in `main()`.

14.2.5 Terminate the Run within MYSUB
```
exit(999);
```
`999` can be replaced by any Integer. The Value so returned is accessible by DOS in the form of `ERRORLEVEL`.
Or:
```
abort();
```

14.2.6 Can a Subroutine be created and maintained as a separate Program?
Yes.

14.2.7 Can Statements in the Body be Executed as part of the Main Program?

No. Cannot Branch or Run into a Subroutine Body. It can only be Executed by invoking the Subroutine.

14.2.8 Can two separate Subroutines share part or all of the same Body?

No (but see 14.2.4). Statements to be "shared" should be placed in a third Subroutine to be called by each of the first two.

14.2.9 Can a Subroutine be invoked within the Body of another Subroutine?

Yes.

14.2.10 What restrictions are there on doing this?

In the event of recursion (e.g. as a result of a Subroutine calling itself) then the processor stack needs to be large enough to prevent stack overflow.

14.2.11 Can a Subroutine be invoked within its own Body?

Yes. Localise all Variables used internally to avoid conflict.

14.3 Data used internally by a Subroutine

When a Subroutine is called, there is the opportunity to communicate data between the calling Program and the Body of the Subroutine by means of Arguments and returned Values. Arguments are specified externally to the Body, but behave like Localised Variables. This section treats the various ways of specifying such Arguments, as well as Localised Variables and the returned Value. Sample Subroutines are given to perform simple tasks by way of illustration, and the form of calling them is shown.

The proposed ANSI standard offers a new way of specifying Arguments and the returned Value, viz. "function prototyping". In what follows the new way will be given first, followed by the old way. Zortech C accepts either, but except for interfacing with pre-existing (ported) code the new way should be used.

14.3.1 Specify X to be an Integer Argument of MYSUB

```
mysub(int x)
{...}
```

or:

```
mysub(x)
int x;
{...}
```

14.3.2 Specify X to be a Non-Integer Argument of MYSUB

```
mysub(double x)
{...}
```
or:
```
mysub(x)
double x;
{...}
```
(float) may be used instead of (double), but the proposed ANSI Standard recommends against its use. Obviously definition and invocations should nevertheless match, using one or the other.

14.3.3 Specify Y to be a String Argument of MYSUB

```
mysub(int x, char *y)
{...}
```
or:
```
mysub(x,y)
int x;
char *y;
{...}
```

14.3.4 Specify Y to be an Array Argument of MYSUB

As in 14.3.3, replacing (char) with the required Type of Array Entry, e.g. (int).
The following are also possible:
```
mysub(int x, int y[])
{...}
```
or:
```
mysub(x,y)
int x;
int y[];
{...}
```

14.3.5 What range of Types can an Argument possess?

All Numeric Types and (char), including those defined by typedef, and Pointers to the same. The proposed ANSI Standard also allows Structures.

14.3.6 Specify V to be Localised within the Body of MYSUB

```
mysub(int x)
{
int v;
...
}
```
or:
```
mysub(x)
```

```
int x;
{
int v;
...
}
```

14.3.7 What Types of data can be Localised?
All Types.

14.3.8 Do Local Variables differ from Arguments in the Body of MYSUB?
No. Essentially the only difference is that an Argument starts off with the Value the Subroutine has been called with, whereas a Local Variable needs to be initialised. Arguments can be reassigned and used as Local Variables.

14.3.9 Return the chief Value computed by the Subroutine MYSUB to the Point of Invocation
```
z = mysub(x); /* point of invocation */
...
int mysub(int x)
{
...
return 99;
}
```
(Old way). Replace: `int mysub(int x)` by:
```
int mysub(x)
int x;
```
Note that:
```
int mysub(...)
```
declares the returned Value to have the Type (int). The Type (int) may be replaced by any other Type, including (struct), (union) and (void), but excluding Functions and Arrays. If omitted, (int) is assumed, e.g. as in:
```
mysub(...)
```
99 may be replaced by any Integer, or a Value of the same Type as `mysub()`.

14.3.10 Can a Subroutine return more than one computed Value?
Yes,
(a) by combining the Values into a single Structure and using the technique of 14.3.9
(b) by defining Arguments to be Pointers to the required Type of Value, rather than actual Values, and invoking `mysub()` as follows:

```
mysub(&x, &y); /* Invocation -- will alter x and y */
...
mysub(int *v1, int *v2)
{
...
*v1 = 99;
*v2 = 987;
}
```
(Old way). Replace: mysub(int *v1, int *v2) by:
```
mysub(v1,v2)
int *v1, *v2;
```

14.3.11 Can a Function be computed by means of a Subroutine Body?

Yes. See for example 14.3.9.

Note that there is essentially no difference between a Subroutine and a user-specified Function in C. Both are called "functions". Thus mysub(), defined as:
```
mysub(int x) {...}
```
or (old way) as:
```
mysub(x) int x; {...}
```
is assumed to return a Value of Type (int) and may be invoked in either fashion:
```
z = mysub(123);
```
or:
```
mysub(123);
```
In the latter case the returned Value is simply discarded. If the returned Value is never required, mysub() may be declared as follows:
```
void mysub(int x) {...}
```
or (old way) as:
```
void mysub(x) int x; {...}
```

14.3.12 Specify a Subroutine MYSUB to output the Nth of a list of 3 messages
```
mysub(int n)
{
 static char *m[] = {
 "",
 "\nMessage No. 1",
 "\nMessage No. 2",
 "\nMessage No. 3",
 }; /* NB: Semicolon needed here */
 puts(m[n]);
}
```

14.3.13 Invoke MYSUB to output message no. 2
```
mysub(2);
```

14.3.14 Specify a Subroutine MYSUB to output TYPE A NONZERO NUMBER and accept only a valid reply
```
int mysub(void)
{
int r = 0;
while (r==0) {
 puts("TYPE A NONZERO NUMBER");
 scanf("%d",&r); flushall();
 }
return r;
}
```
Without `flushall()` the Program malfunctions if a bad Character (e.g. a Letter) is typed in.

14.3.15 Invoke MYSUB putting the reply into the Variable U
```
u = mysub();
```

14.3.16 Specify a Subroutine MYSUB to output TYPE A PAIR OF NONZERO NUMBERS and accept only valid replies
```
mysub(int *q, int *r)
{
*q = *r = 0;
while ((*q==0)||(*r==0)) {
 puts("TYPE A PAIR OF NONZERO NUMBERS");
 scanf("%d %d",q,r); flushall();
 }
}
```
(Old way). Replace: `mysub2(int *q, int *r)` by:
```
mysub(q,r)
int *q, *r;
```

14.3.17 Invoke MYSUB putting the replies into the Variables U and V
```
mysub(&u,&v);
```

14.3.18 Specify a Subroutine MYSUB to compute (X+Y)/2
```
double mysub(double x, double y)
{
return (x+y)/2;
}
```
or:

```
double mysub(x,y)
double x, y;
{
return (x+y)/2;
}
```

Note: if this declaration of `mysub()` appears after `main()` then an external declaration preceding `main()` is needed, e.g.
```
double mysub();
```

14.3.19 Invoke MYSUB with the Values of U and V as Arguments and put the result in Z
```
z = mysub(u,v);
```

14.4 Pass an Argument to a Subroutine at the Point of Invocation

This section treats the ways of specifying Values or Variables of various Types in the calling Statement as the Subroutine's Argument.

14.4.1 Pass a Constant, e.g. 2.54
```
mysub(2.54);
```

14.4.2 Pass the current Value of a Variable Z
```
mysub(z);
```

14.4.3 Identify Variable Z for the Subroutine to alter its Value
```
mysub(&z); /* Point of Invocation */
...
mysub(int *x) {...} /* Definition of mysub() */
```
Old way (definition only):
```
mysub(x) int x; {...} /* Definition of mysub() */
```

14.4.4 Pass the result of an Expression (X+Y)/2
```
mysub((x+y)/2);
```

14.4.5 Is passing a Constant or a Variable a special case of passing an Expression?
Yes, provided the Argument is specified to be a Value, not a Pointer.

14.4.6 Pass the Function MYFUN which is to be invoked within the Body of the Subroutine itself
```
double myfun(int); /* This line is needed (see
   14.3.18) */
...
mysub4(99,myfun); /* Point of Invocation */
```

```
/* calls myfun with Argument 99 */
...
mysub4( int u, double (*f)() )
{
 double z;
 z = (*f)(u); printf("%f",z);
}
...
double myfun(int u)
{
 return (double) u*u; /* squares its arg */
}
```

Or (old way):

```
double myfun(); /* This line is needed, see
   14.3.18 */
...
mysub4(99,myfun); /* Point of Invocation */
/* calls myfun with Argument 99 */
...
mysub4(u,f)
int u;
double (*f)();
{
 double z;
 z = (*f)(u); printf("%f",z);
}
...
double myfun(u)
int u;
{
 return (double) u*u; /* squares its arg */
}
```

14.5 Specify a new Function

See 14.1.2 for the rationale of a Function and how C supports it.

14.5.1 What restrictions are there on naming a Function?
Any valid unused Identifier can be employed.

14.5.2 Specify the Function sinc X to be (sin X)/X
```
double sinc(double x)
{
 return sin(x)/x;
}
```

or:
```
double sinc(x)
double x;
{
  return sin(x)/x;
}
```
In practice such a simple Function would be defined by a Macro (see 14.6) e.g.
```
#define sinc(x) sin(x)/x
```

14.5.3 Specify the Function MYFUN to be (X+Y)/2
See 14.3.18.
In practice such a simple Function would be defined by a Macro (see 14.6.2) e.g.
```
#define myfun(x,y) (x+y)/2
```

14.5.4 Specify a Function MYFUN whose Value is computed by a Subroutine Body
See 14.5.2 and all those examples in 14.3 which return Values.

14.5.5 Are Parentheses needed round the Argument(s)?
Yes, e.g.
```
sin(x);
```

14.6 Specify a Macro

See 14.1.3 for the rationale of a Macro and how C supports it.

14.6.1 Specify a Macro MAC(X) to be equivalent to (X+1)/2
```
#define mac(x) ((x)+1)/2
```

14.6.2 Specify a Macro MAC(X,Y) to be equivalent to (X+Y)/2
```
#define mac(x,y) (x+y)/2
```
To allow safe Macro-expansion if Expressions are to be used as Arguments, enclose the symbolic Arguments, x and y, in Parentheses, e.g.
```
#define mac(x,y) ((x)+(y))/2
```

14.6.3 Are Parentheses needed round the Argument(s)?
Yes, e.g.
```
mac(u+1,v+1);
```

15

Syntax: broad features of the Language

This chapter describes the broad features of the C Language, dwelling on those Syntax conventions which cause the most problems to the casual programmer transferring between Languages. Topics covered are the Character Set, Reserved Words, valid Identifiers, Comments, Lowercase and Uppercase, spacing Characters and Terminators, the usage of Special Characters (#!%^&*-_+=\|/~<>?), Apostrophe, Quote and the treatment of Literal Constants, the bracketing symbols () [] {} and the essential structure of a Program.

15.1 Tokens in the Program

Tokens are Characters or strings of Characters which the Language Processor treats as unsplittable. For a fuller definition see Appendix A. What C treats as a Token is summarised in 15.1.2.

15.1.1 What is the Character Set for a Program (excluding Literal Constants)?

Letters (A...Z a...z)
Digits (0...9)
Space, Tab, Carriage Return, Newline
Parentheses, Square Brackets and Braces () [] {}
Punctuation (.,;:"')
Special Characters (#!%^&*-_+=\|/~<>?)

15.1.2 What is the set of valid Tokens?

Parentheses: ()
Square Brackets: []
Braces: {}
Identifiers (see 2.2) e.g.: abc ABC AbcDef x X x12 x_y_z
Reserved Words: (see 15.1.4)
Operators (prefix): - ~ ! * & # ++ --
Operators (suffix): ++ -- () (...)
Operators (infix): + - * / % , & | ^
> < && || -> ?:
+= -= *= /= %= <<= >>= &= ^= |=
<= >= == !=

Separators and Terminators: Period (.), Comma (,), Semicolon
(;), Colon (:), Apostrophe ('), Quote ("), Comment
/*...*/, Space, Tab, Newline, Carriage Return.

Numerals: 123 123u 123L
```
 1.23E+21 1.23E-21 1.23E21 1.23 1.0
 1.23e+21 1.23e-21 1.23e21 0377 0xFF 0xff
 '\n' '\t' '\b' '\r' '\f' '\0' '\\'
```
'\x...' (Integer Hex Numeral)
'\...' (Integer Octal Numeral)
'a' (Integer ASCII Code)

15.1.3 What constitutes an Identifier?
First Character must be a Letter (A...Z a...z) or Underscore (_).
Any sequence of Characters may follow, chosen from the Letters
(A...Z a...z), the Digits (0...9) and Underscore (_).
Maximum length of Identifier is 127 Characters.

15.1.4 What is the set of Reserved Words?
```
auto break case char const continue default do
double else entry enum extern far float for goto
if int long near register return short signed
sizeof static struct switch typedef union
unsigned void volatile while
```

15.1.5 What constitutes a Comment?
Initial Token /* followed by any sequence of Characters including
Space, Tab, Carriage Return and Newline until the Token */ is
encountered.

15.1.6 Is Lowercase recognised in Reserved Words?
Yes, Reserved Words MUST be in Lowercase or else they are not
recognised.

15.1.7 Is Lowercase recognised in Identifiers?
Yes.

15.1.8 Is Lowercase treated like equivalent Uppercase?
No.

15.1.9 Is Uppercase mandatory for any purpose?
No. However by convention Uppercase is used for Named Constants,
e.g.
```
 #define TRUE 1
```

15.2 Blank Separators in the Program

C accepts so-called "white space" Characters, Carriage Return, Newline and Tab, as Syntactically equivalent to Space, serving only to separate Tokens. They may be present only for legibility or appearance. Division of the Program into lines is irrelevant to the Syntax.

15.2.1 Is the Space Character (ASCII 32) ever required to separate Tokens?

Yes. Space (or Tab, Newline, Carriage Return) is essential for separating consecutive Reserved Words or Identifiers, e.g.

```
else if ...
```

or:

```
sizeof y;
```

15.2.2 Is the Space Character (ASCII 32) itself a Token?
No.

15.2.3 Are consecutive Spaces treated as a single Space?
Yes, except within Literal Constants, where all Spaces are honoured, e.g.
```
"   >>>"
```

15.2.4 Is Tab (ASCII 9) always treated like Space?
Yes.

15.2.5 Is Carriage Return (ASCII 13) always treated like Space?
Yes.

15.3 Special Characters used as Statement Terminators

Statements must be explicitly terminated (see 15.3.3). Individual Expressions may serve as Statements and be separated by Comma (,). This use of Comma (,) is however generally reserved for the for Statement.

15.3.1 Are line endings ignored in a Program?
Yes.

15.3.2 Is Carriage Return a Statement Terminator?
No.

15.3.3 Can Statements be terminated by other Characters besides Carriage Return?
Yes. A simple Statement cannot be terminated by Carriage Return and MUST be terminated by Semicolon (;) and a compound Statement by Right Brace (}).

15.3.4 Write two Statements on the same line to increment both X and Y

```
x++; y++;
```
or:
```
x++, y++;
```
See remark about Comma in 15.3.

15.4 Other special Characters

There is no accepted standard between different Languages as to the meaning of "special" Characters. This serves to heighten the illegibility of C Programs to newcomers, even if they can program already. This section is intended to allow quick cross-reference between other Languages and C.

15.4.1 Is Period (.) used to represent the Decimal Point?
Yes.

15.4.2 Is Period (.) used for any other purpose?
Yes, to designate a Term in a Structure. Thus if x is a Term in the Structure: `point`, it would be accessed thus:
```
z = point.x;
```
or:
```
point.x = 99;
```

15.4.3 Is Comma (,) used to separate the Arguments in a Function or Subroutine invocation?
Yes.

15.4.4 Is Comma (,) used for any other purpose?
As a Separator of Identifiers in multi-Identifier declarations, e.g.
```
double x,y;
```

As a Separator of Constants in an Array or Structure initialisation construct, e.g.
```
int a[] = {1, 2, 3, 4, 5};
```

As a Separator of Arguments in a Subroutine or Function invocation, e.g.
```
mysub(x+1,y+2);
```

As a subsidiary Separator of Statements (actually a trivially-acting arithmetic Operator) in the `for`-construct, e.g.
```
for (i=0,j=1; i<N; i++,j++) {...}
```

15.4.5 Is Semicolon (;) used for any purpose?
As the Statement Terminator. See 15.3.3.

15.4.6 Is Hyphen (-) used to express arithmetic subtraction?
Yes.

15.4.7 Does a leading Hyphen (-) in a Numeric Expression signify Negation?

Yes.

15.4.8 Is Hyphen (-) used for any other purpose?
In various decrementing constructs, e.g.
```
x--; y = --x; y -= 1;
```
Note also its use in the Operator: ->

15.4.9 Is Plus (+) used to express arithmetic addition?
Yes.

15.4.10 Is Plus (+) used for any other purpose?
In various incrementing constructs, e.g.
```
x++; y = ++x; y += 1;
```

15.4.11 Is Slash (/) used to express arithmetic division?
Yes.

15.4.12 Is Slash (/) used for any other purpose?
No, not by itself.
Note however its use in the Comment Delimiters: /* ... */

15.4.13 Is Asterisk (*) used for arithmetic multiplication?
Yes.

15.4.14 Is Asterisk (*) used for any other purpose?
To declare a Pointer or cast a Pointer Expression, e.g.
```
char *p;
```
or:
```
p = (char *) q;
```
Note also its use in the Comment Delimiters: /* ... */

15.4.15 Is Equals (=) used to express Variable Assignment?
Yes.

15.4.16 Is Equals (=) used for any other purpose?
In incrementing or decrementing constructs, e.g.
```
y-=2; y+=1;
```
Note also the Logical Operators: == != >= <=

101

e.g.
```
if (x==y) {...}
```

15.4.17 Are Ampersand (&) At (@) Backslash (\) Bar (|) Caret (^) Dollar ($) Hash (#) Percent (%) Query (?) Shriek (!) Tilde (~) and Underscore (_) Tokens having particular meanings?

Ampersand (&) is the Operator to yield a Pointer to the Value of a given Variable, e.g.
```
void *p; ...; p = &z;
```
or:
```
scanf("%d",&n); /* needed to alter n itself */
```
Ampersand (&) is also the Bitwise AND Operator, e.g.
```
z = z&0x7fff;
```
Note also the AND Logical Operator (&&) e.g.
```
if ((x==0)&&(y==0)) {...}
```

At (@) and Dollar ($) are not used at all.

Backslash (\) is used to express special Characters inside Literal Constants, e.g. Newline in:
```
printf("\nHELLO WORLD");
```
or Carriage Return in:
```
if (c=='\r') {...}
```

Bar (|) is the Bitwise OR Operator, e.g.
```
z = z|0x7fff;
```
Note also the OR Logical Operator (||) e.g.
```
if ((x==0)||(y==0)) {...}
```

Caret (^) is the Bitwise XOR Operator e.g.
```
b = b^0x00ff;
```

Hash (#) is the prefix to a Compiler directive, e.g.
```
#include <stdio.h>
```
or:
```
#define A 123
```
or:
```
#ifdef A
...
#endif
```

Percent (%) is the Remainder Operator, e.g.
```
parity = j%2;
```
Note also Percent (%) used as the "escape character" inside the formatting String used by printf(), scanf() and their relatives, to specify the insertion of a formatted Value, e.g.
```
printf("The answers are %d and %d",x,y);
```
See Appendix D for a full list of formatting constructs using Percent (%) in printf() and scanf().

Query (?) is used in conjunction with Colon (:) in the Conditional Assignment construct e.g.:

```
z = (x==0) ? y : x;
```

Shriek (!) is the NOT Logical Operator, e.g.

```
if (!z==99) {...}
```

Note also the Relational Operator "not-equals" (!=), e.g.

```
if (z!=0) {...}
```

Tilde (~) is the Bitwise-NOT Operator (flips all Bits in an Integer).

Underscore (_) is a valid Character in an Identifier.

15.4.18 Do >= and => both signify "greater-than-or-equal-to"?

No, only >= does so.

15.4.19 Do <= and =< both signify "less-than-or-equal-to"?

No, only <= does so.

15.4.20 Do <> and >< both signify "not-equal-to"?

Neither does. Use: !=.

15.5 Apostrophe and Quote

Both balanced Quotes and balanced Apostrophes can be used to delimit Literal Constants, but the meaning is different. See 3.1. An escape Character, Backslash (\) is reserved for inserting Quote, Apostrophe or other problematic Characters into Literal Constants.

15.5.1 Are balanced Quotes ("...") used to delimit Literal Constants?

Yes. (A trailing Null character is automatically appended to the Value in Memory)

15.5.2 Can final Quote (") be omitted at the end of a line?

No.

15.5.3 Are balanced Apostrophes ('...') used to delimit Literal Constants?

Yes, but only to specify Numeric Values, e.g.

```
'A'   --the ASCII Value of Letter (A) (Hex: 41)
'AB'  --2 Bytes: Hex: 4142
'\n'  --Carriage Return
'\''  --the Apostrophe Character
'\"'  --the Quote Character
```

15.5.4 Display the Literal Constant IT'S OK
```
puts("IT'S OK");
```
or:
```
puts("IT\'S OK");
```

15.5.5 Display the Literal Constant THE "MERMAID"
```
puts("THE \"MERMAID\"");
```

15.5.6 Is Quote (") used for any other purpose?
No.

15.5.7 Is Apostrophe (') used for any other purpose?
No.

15.6 Use of Parentheses (...), Square Brackets [...] and Braces {...}

Parentheses (...) are used conventionally. Square Brackets [...] are used to delimit Array Indexes. Braces { ... } are used to delimit Blocks of Statements, including Subroutine Bodies and the Program main().

15.6.1 Are Parentheses used conventionally to guide the order of evaluation of an Expression, e.g. (A+B)*C?
Yes.

15.6.2 Can closing Parentheses ...) be omitted at ends of lines?
No. Parentheses must always balance within a Statement.

15.6.3 Are Parentheses (...) used to delimit the Argument list in Function invocations?
Yes.

15.6.4 Are Parentheses (...) used to delimit the Argument list in Subroutine invocations?
Yes.

15.6.5 Are Parentheses (...) used to delimit Array Indexes?
No. Use Square Brackets [...].

15.6.6 Are Parentheses (...) used for any other purpose?
To override Operator Precedence, or to cast an Expression to a different Type, e.g.
```
p = (char *) q;
```

15.6.7 Are Square Brackets [...] used to delimit Array Indexes?

Yes, e.g.
```
a[i+1]
```
or:
```
matrix[5][3]
```

15.6.8 Are Square Brackets [...] used for any other purpose?

No.

15.6.9 Are Braces {...} used for any particular purpose?

To collect Statements into Blocks, or compound Statements, in struct and union declarations, and to initialise multi-valued Variables, e.g.
```
int nnn[] = {1, 2, 3, 4, 5};
```

15.7 Program structure

Programs consist of a sequence of Subroutines, each consisting of a Header and a Body, a single (possibly nested) Block. There is at most one Subroutine called main(), which is entered when the Program is Run from DOS. Variables can be declared at the beginning of a Body and are local to that Subroutine. Variables can also be declared outside all Bodies, these are called "external" and are visible to all the Subroutine Bodies they precede. This section describes a typical Program, as well as exhibiting the most primitive Program to display a message.

15.7.1 How are Statements collected into Blocks?

By enclosing a sequence of consecutive Statements in Braces { ... }.

15.7.2 Is there a mandatory or usual Terminator for a Program?

The entire Program Body forms a single Block. Hence the outermost balancing right Brace (}) of the Main Program, or the final Subroutine, terminates the Program listing, viz:
```
...
}
```

15.7.3 Is there a mandatory or usual form of Header for the Main Program?
```
main()
```
or, to accept Arguments from the DOS Command line:
```
main(argc, argv)
```

Note that this Phrase is not followed by Semicolon (;) but by the Program Body between Braces { ... }

15.7.4 Is there a mandatory or usual form of commencing a Program?

Yes, with Comment(s) describing the purpose of the Program, e.g.
```
/* Sample Program */
```

15.7.5 What is the structure of a typical Program?
```
/* Sample Program */
#include <stdio.h>
#include <math.h>
...
#define TRUE 1
#define FALSE 0
...
double fn1(double u); /* forward reference to:
  fn1() */
...
main()
{
  ...
}
sub1(x,y)
int x;
char *y;
{
  ...
}
double fn1(double u)
{
  ...
}
```
Note that sub1() has an old-style declaration, but fn1() has an ANSI Standard declaration employing "function prototyping". Either may still be used with ANSI Standard Compilers.

15.7.6 What parts of this Program structure are mandatory?
```
main() {...}
```

15.7.7 Exhibit the simplest Program to display HELLO WORLD
```
#include <stdio.h>
main()
{
  printf("HELLO WORLD\n");
}
```

15.7.8 Can more than one Program be specified in a given Program File?

Yes, but only one called `main()`.

15.7.9 Is a Program File created or updated using a preferred Editor?

Yes, with the ZED Editor (when using Zortech C).

15.7.10 Can a Program File be created or updated using an ASCII File Editor, e.g. EDLIN?

Yes. Most vendors' C Compilers accept Program Files which are conventional ASCII (text) Files. Most however also provide a text Editor with the basic C System. Zortech provides ZED.

Appendix A

Standard C3S Terms for programming concepts

The words below have special meanings in the C3S classification system. They describe programming tasks but are not specific to the Language presented in this book.

Wherever such terms are used, they are capitalised. Wherever such a word is used without being capitalised, it is to be understood informally. Thus a Value is defined as "an item of data ...(etc.)" and Number is "A Value representing a numeral...(etc.)", but "item of data" and "numeral" carry their informal meanings. Likewise the C3S term, Number, is not intended in, say, "a number of alternatives".

Address A Value specifying a Memory location.

Alphanumeric One of the Characters a ... z A ... Z 0 ... 9

{Alt-A} ({Alt-B}, {Alt-C}, ...) A Keystroke combination in which A is struck whilst holding down the Key labelled Alt.

Ampersand The Character ASCII 38 (&).

Ancillary Key A non-Character Key which modifies the action of some other Key, viz. {Shift-}, {Ctl-}, {Alt-}, {Caps Lock}, {Num Lock}.

Apostrophe The Character ASCII 39 (').

Application A suite of one or more Executable Programs together with their associated data Files.

Argument An Identifier or Expression in a Statement specifying some Address or Value to be passed to a given Function or Subroutine when it is invoked.

Array A Variable consisting of several indexable Terms, each possessing a separate Value (usually) all of the same Type.

ASCII American Standard Code for Information Intechange. A Teleprinter Code of 7-Bit Values for Characters plus various reserved codes, an 8-Bit adaptation of which is used by DOS, but nevertheless still called ASCII.

ASCII File A File consisting entirely of ASCII codes, therefore legible by means of the DOS Commands: TYPE and PRINT, and maintainable by using the DOS Editor: EDLIN.

Assignment The act of placing a given Value into a given Variable.

Asterisk The Character ASCII 42 (*).

At The Character ASCII 64 (@).

Backslash The Character ASCII 92 (\).

Backspace The Character ASCII 8.

{Backspace} The Key labelled <-Del, or |<-, which either undoes the previous Keystroke or generates a Backspace Character.

Bar The Character ASCII 124 (|).

Base The act of attaching a Variable to a particular Memory Location without destroying its contents, thereby causing the Variable to assume some Value corresponding to its Type.

Beep The Character ASCII 7. When output to the Screen or a Line Printer, does not take up a Character position, but instead sounds the Bell.

Bell An audible Device attached to the Screen or a Printer which is activated by attempting to output the Beep Character.

Binary A convention which represents a Numeric Constant to the base 2, using the Digits 0 and 1 only. Also used to represent the Bit Pattern of a Value in Memory. (See Octal, Hex).

Binary Digit The Digits 0 and 1, used to represent either a Truth Value or the state of a given Bit at some point in time.

Bit A single 2-state Device, being the smallest unit of Memory, or its image on some given storage medium.

Bit Pattern A sequence of Binary Digits describing the contents of Memory starting at a given Address.

Block A syntactically grouped collection of Statements, treatable as a (compound) Statement.

Body The collection of Statements specifying the action of a given Program or Subroutine (See Header).

Box A rectangular graphic figure.

Branch The act of Executing some other specified Statement in the Program instead of the Statement which naturally follows on.

{Break} The Key labelled Break.

Byte A Hardware-supported Memory Location of 8 Bits, conventionally numbered 0, 1, 2, ..., 7 from the left.

Calendar A Device registering the current date.

{Caps Lock} The Key labelled Caps Lock, causing unshifted Letters to become Uppercase.

Caret The Character ASCII 94 (^).

Carriage Return The Character ASCII 13.

Character The Value of a 1-Byte coded item of data in Memory.

Character Key A Key that places a code in the Keyboard buffer.

Character Set The set of Characters employed for specifying a Program in the given Language.

Circle A circular graphic figure.

Clock A Device registering the current time-of-day.

Closed The state of a File in which neither the System nor the Program is maintaining any working reference to it in Memory.

Colon The Character ASCII 58 (:).

Comma The Character ASCII 44 (,).

Command A coded specification of some action requested to be done by the System.

Comment A Statement the contents of which the System ignores.

Condition An Expression whose Value is either True or False

Condition Statement A Program Statement governed by a Condition, which when Executed acts only when the Condition is True.

Constant The specification of some Value which is fixed in the Program and cannot be altered during a Run.

{Ctl-A} ({Ctl-B}, {Ctl-C} ...) A Keystroke combination in which A is struck whilst holding down the Key labelled Ctl.

Cursor The position on the Screen at which the next typed Character will appear.

Decimal A convention which represents a Numeric Constant to the base 10, using the Digits 0, 1, ... 9.

Decimal Point A Period used to mark the units Digit in the conventional decimal representation of a Non-Integer Constant. This convention is NOT universal, Period (.) being replaced by Comma (,) in some countries. However few computer Languages support the Comma convention.

{Del} The Key labelled Del, which deletes a Character just typed.

Device A piece of Hardware capable of generating an Event or being activated by the Program at Runtime.

Digit One of the Characters: 0...9.

Directory A System File used by DOS to identify a subsidiary collection of other Files.

Disk A Device for storing Files on a magnetic medium. Identified to the DOS System by a single Letter (A ... Z). A built-in "hard disk" is usually Disk C (See Drive).

Diskette A removable Disk (See Disk, Drive).

DOS The operating system: PCDOS_ or MS-DOS_.

{Down} The Key labelled with a downward arrow.

Drive A Device for reading and writing a (fixed) Disk or a Diskette.

Editor A System utility to enable the contents of a Program or data File to be created or changed interactively.

Ellipse An elliptical graphic figure.

{End} The Key labelled End.

End-of-File The state of the System arising from attempting to read past the last Record of some File.

{Enter} The Key labelled Enter.

Entry Point The Statement in a given Subroutine Body which is the first to be Executed when the Subroutine is invoked.

EOF The Character ASCII 26, which signals the End-of-File of a Text File.

Equals The Character ASCII 61 (=).

Error One of several classified states of the System when it Fails, e.g. whilst attempting to Run a bad Program.

Escape The Character ASCII 27.

Escape Key {Esc} The Key labelled Esc, which generates an Escape Character, but whose action is Software-dependent.

Event A Hardware occurrence which can be detected by a Running Program.

Exclamation Mark See Shriek.

Execute To be in the process of performing (successful) Execution (See Fail).

Execution The successful carrying out of the Hardware activity specified by a Program or one of its Statements.

Expression A Phrase within a Statement which specifies a Value, or how a Value is to be computed when the Statement is Executed. A trivial Expression may consist of a single Constant or a single (Identifier of a) Variable.

{f1} ({f2}, {f3}, ...) The Key labelled f1. (Similarly f2, f3, ...).

Fail Refusal by the System to Execute a Statement.

False The Logical Constant which represents some given Condition having been NOT satisfied at some given point in time. (See True).

Field A measured portion of a Memory Location, or its corresponding image within a File Record, or row of the Screen.

File An updatable collection of data stored on a Diskette and managed by DOS, of which portions can be read into (written out from) Memory.

File Number An Integer by which a Program refers to an Open File.

File Pointer The (System-maintained) start of the next portion of an Open File to be read into (written out from) Memory.

Fixed Point A Non-Integer Type, represented to a pre-determined precision which yields the number of Digits to the right of the Decimal Point (See Non-Integer, Floating Point).

Floating Point A Non-Integer Type, represented to a pre-determined precision which yields the number of significant Digits in the specified Number (See Non-Integer, Fixed Point).

Form Feed The Character ASCII 12, which causes an ASCII Printer to do a paper-throw or clears the Screen.

Function An Expression consisting of an Identifier and possibly one or more Arguments, the (Runtime) Value of which is specified elsewhere in the Program.

Function Key One of the Keys labelled {f1}, {f2}, ...

Hardware A component of the System which communicates with the rest of the System electronically or mechanically. See Device, Software.

Hash The Character ASCII 35 (#).

Header Part of the specification of a Program or Subroutine that determines how it should be invoked (See Body).

Hexadecimal (Hex) A convention which represents a Numeric Constant to the base 16, using Hex Digits. Also used to represent the Bit Pattern of a Value in Memory since each Hex Digit stands for the setting of four consecutive Bits, and a pair of Hex Digits the contents of one Byte.

Hex Digit The Characters 0, 1, ..., 9, a, b, c, d, e, f. (See Hex).

{Home} The Key labelled Home.

Horizontal Tab The Character ASCII 9 (See Tab).

Hyphen The Character ASCII 45 (-).

I.D. Short for ''Identifier'', but in this case usually standing for a Number used as the (System-defined) Name of some data item, e.g. File I.D.

Identifier A syntactically governed sequence of Characters for use as a Name within a Statement or Command.

{Ins} The Key labelled Ins, which the System can recognise to toggle Insert Mode.

Index A Value (typically an Integer) used to refer to a given Term of an Array.

Integer A Type capable of representing a whole-number only, whether Positive, Zero or Negative.

Key A Hardware Device to input an Event to the System when manually depressed.

Keyboard A Device having a collection of Keys.

Keyboard Buffer An internal queue to register Keystrokes pending their acceptance by the System.

Keystroke The act of depressing a Character Key.

Label A Phrase (typically an Identifier or a Number) to identify a given Program Statement from within some other Statement.

Language A Syntax and a collection of conventions for writing a Program.

{Left} The Key labelled with a leftward arrow.

Letter One of the Characters A ... Z a ... z.

Line Feed The Character ASCII 10. See also Newline.

Line Printer A Device for printing entire lines of text on paper.

Literal Constant A Phrase specifying a Character or String Value in a direct manner by setting down the actual Character contents in a Statement.

Localised An Identifier whose meaning is defined only within a given Block, or the Body of a given Subroutine, and can be freely re-used elsewhere in the Program.

Logical Constant A Constant which is one of the two Values True or False.

Logical Operator An Operator to alter or combine one or more Logical Values.

Logical Value See Truth Value.

Loop The act of repeatedly Executing a Block of Statements in the Program.

Lowercase A Character which is not one of (or a String not containing) the Letters A ... Z.

Macro A construct which specifies the replacement in the Program of each occurrence of a given Identifier (possibly parameterised) with a sequence of Characters, usually an Expression, Statement or collection of Statements.

Main Program The Program which governs the Run, and which does not serve as a Subroutine to any other Program.

Mask A Bit Pattern used as a template in conjunction with Logical Operators for forcing or ignoring the settings of particular Bits.

Masking The construct of employing a Mask to operate directly upon the Bit Pattern of a given Value.

Memory The Device which provides transient general-purpose working storage for all kinds of data.

Memory Location A piece of Memory recognised by the System to be storing a Value.

Name An Identifier applied uniquely to some object within the System or Program, e.g. a Variable, a Constant, a Statement, a Program, a File or a Device.

Negative The state of a Numeric Value being less than Zero.

Newline The Character ASCII 10. (See also Line Feed).

Non-Integer A Type which represents a Number having a fractional part, even though this part may be Zero. (See Fixed Point, Floating Point).

Null The Character ASCII 0.

Null String A String of length Zero.

Number A Value representing a numeral, e.g. 1, -2, 1.56, 1.2E+15.

Numeral A Phrase specifying a Number as a String of Characters.

Numeric The Type of a Number.

{Num Lock} The Key labelled Num Lock, which toggles the numeric keypad between numeric mode and cursor key mode.

Octal A convention which represents a Numeric Constant to the base 8, using the Digits 0, 1, ..., 7. Also used to represent the Bit Pattern of a Value in Memory since each Octal Digit stands for the setting of three consecutive bits.

Offset A Convention for specifying an Address in Memory by means of a count of Bytes from the beginning of the containing Segment. The first Byte of a Segment is at Offset 0. (See Segment).

Open The state of a File in which the System is maintaining a working reference to it for the purpose of reading or writing its data.

Operator A Token which specifies some modification to an associated item of data, e.g. -A, or the combination of two such items, e.g. A-B, A*B, etc.

Pen A Device for selecting a Point on the Screen (a "light pen" or a "mouse").

Percent The Character ASCII 37 (%).

Period The Character ASCII 46 (.).

{PgDn} The Key labelled PgDn.

{PgUp} The Key labelled PgUp.

Phrase A recognisable element of a Statement, e.g. a Constant, an Expression, an Operator or a Condition.

Pi The ratio of radius to circumference of a circle.

Pixel One of the array of picture-cells, the smallest switchable elements of the Screen display. Shows a coloured (or darkened) dot.

Plus The Character ASCII 43 (+).

Point The co-ordinates of a given spatial location on the Screen, Rounded to address the nearest Pixel.

Pointer A Type representing an Address in Memory.

Point of Invocation The Statement which invokes a given Subroutine.

Polyline A graphic figure consisting of a non-branching chain or loop of straight lines.

Port A standardised electrical connection between the computer and some external Device, usually a Printer.

Positive The state of a Numeric Value being Zero or more.

Precision The maximum number of significant digits that a given Type of Numeric Variable can register.

Printer See Line Printer.

Program A legible specification of some desired computer activity written in the Language concerned.

Prompt A visible (or audible) signal during a Run, or an Interactive Session, inviting Keyboard input.

{PrtSc} The Key labelled PrtSc.

Query The Character ASCII 63 (?).

Quit The act of terminating a Run or an Interactive Session.

Quote The Character ASCII 34 (").

Record One of perhaps several items of data in a File which the Program handles as a simple or complex Value (typically a String or a Structure).

Reserved Word An otherwise syntactically valid Identifier which is reserved for use only as a Language construct. In many computer Languages the word: if is a Reserved Word.

{Return} The Key labelled RETURN, or with a bent arrow, which generates a Carriage Return Character.

{Right} The Key labelled with a rightward arrow.

Rounding The conversion of a Non-Integer to the nearest Integer above or below.

Run The Execution of a given Program.

Runtime The interval during which a given Program is being Executed.

Screen The main Device which echoes Keystrokes and provides a transient display for miscellaneous data.

Segment A Hardware-supported block of 64K (65536) Bytes in Memory. (See Offset).

Semicolon The Character ASCII 59 (;).

Separator A Character used to separate adjacent Tokens, Identifiers, Phrases in a Statement, or adjacent Statements.

{Shift-A} ({Shift-B}, {Shift-C}, ...) A Keystroke combination in which A (B, C ...) is struck whilst holding down one or other of the two Shift Keys. The result with Letters is normally to generate Uppercase Characters.

Shriek The Character ASCII 33 (!).

Slash The Character ASCII 47 (/).

Software A component of the System which exists only as coded signals within the Hardware.

Space The Character ASCII 32.

Space Bar {Space}The wide Key, usually unmarked, at the bottom of the Keyboard, which generates a Space Character.

Statement A syntactically self-contained element of a Program, typically occupying one line.

Straight Line A graphic figure simulating a straight line between two Points.

String A Value consisting of a finite sequence of Characters.

Structure A Variable having a collection of Values of possibly different Types.

Subroutine A subsidiary Program embedded in, or serving, another Program.

Syntax The grammar of what constitutes a valid Phrase, Statement or entire Program.

System The agent which Runs a Program, comprising the computer Hardware, DOS and the Language Processor.

System Clock See Clock.

Tab The Character ASCII 9, which assists in tabulating data in columns and suggests the typewriter action of moving the platen to the next tab-stop.

Tab Key {Tab} The Key labelled Tab, or ->|, which generates a Tab Character, but whose action is Software-dependent.

Task The goal or aim of a Program, or some collection of Statements within it, e.g. to compute or display some Value in a particular way. The Language is said to support a given Task if it enables the Task to be readily specified.

Term An element of an Array, or Structure, having its own particular Value.

Terminator A Character used to terminate a Phrase within a Statement, or else to denote the end of a Statement.

Text File A File consisting of ASCII coded Bytes representing printable Characters, separated into lines. The end of a line is marked by the Characters: Carriage Return + Newline. The end of the File is marked by the EOF Character.

Tilde The Character ASCII 126 (~).

Token The smallest element of a Statement into which it can be broken down without losing its meaning. Typical Tokens are: Identifiers, Numerals, Operators, Parentheses, Separators, Terminators.

True The Logical Constant which represents some given Condition having been satisfied at some given point in time. (See False).

Truncation The conversion of a Non-Integer to an Integer by removal of the fractional part.

Truth Value A Logical Value expressing the state of a Condition at some given point in time, viz. either True or False.

Type The nature of a Value which determines the meaning of its Bit Pattern in Memory, e.g. Character, String, Integer.

Underscore The Character ASCII 95 (_).

{Up} The Key labelled with an upward arrow.

Uppercase A Character which is not one of (or a String not containing) the Letters a ... z.

Value An item of data belonging to a Variable or Constant, or computed by an Expression, corresponding to a particular Bit Pattern in Memory.

Variable An item of data having a fixed Identifier, a Value which can be changed in the course of a Run, and a Type. Some Languages, but not others, allow the Type as well as the Value to change in the course of a Run.

Vertical Tab The Character ASCII 11.

Window A rectangular portion of the Screen within which input and output data can be temporarily confined.

Zero The Value, irrespective of Type, corresponding to the Number 0.

Appendix B

Table of ASCII Characters

Char.No. (Decimal)	1st Digit (Hex)	1st Digits (Octal)	2nd Digit (Octal/Hex) *0 / 2nd Digit (Hex Only) *8	*1 / *9	*2 / *A	*3 / *B	*4 / *C	*5 / *D	*6 / *E	*7 / *F
0-7	0*	00*	NUL	SOH	STX	ETX	EOT	ENQ	ACK	BEL
8-15	0*	01*	BS	HT	NL	VT	FF	CR	SO	SI
16-23	1*	02*	DLE	DC1	DC2	DC3	DC4	NAK	SYN	ETB
24-31	1*	03*	CAN	EM	SUB	ESC	FS	GS	RS	US
32-39	2*	04*	Space	!	Quote	#	$	%	&	Apostrophe
40-47	2*	05*	(	)	*	+	Comma	Hyphen	Period	/
48-55	3*	06*	0	1	2	3	4	5	6	7
56-63	3*	07*	8	9	Colon	Semicolon	<	=	>	?
64-71	4*	010*	@	A	B	C	D	E	F	G
72-79	4*	011*	H	I	J	K	L	M	N	O
80-87	5*	012*	P	Q	R	S	T	U	V	W
88-95	5*	013*	X	Y	Z	[	\	]	Caret	Underscore
96-103	6*	014*	`	a	b	c	d	e	f	g
104-111	6*	015*	h	i	j	k	l	m	n	o
112-119	7*	016*	p	q	r	s	t	u	v	w
120-127	7*	017*	x	y	z	{			}	~	DEL

Notes:

The following Characters have special designations in C, for use between Apostrophes as shown, as Constants of Type (int), or within literal Strings (in which case omit the surrounding Apostrophes):

NL	Newline	'\n'	\	Backslash	'\\'
HT	Horizontal Tab	'\t'	?	Query	'\?'
VT	Vertical Tab	'\v'	'	Apostrophe	'\''
BS	Backspace	'\b'	"	Quote	'\"'
CR	Carriage Return	'\r'	377	Octal Number	'\377'
FF	Form Feed	'\f'	77	Octal Number	'\77'
BEL	Beep	'\a'	7	Octal Number	'\7'
ff	Hex Number	'\xff'	NUL	(Octal) Zero	'\0'

How to use this Table.

The symbol % is in the upper row row 2*, in column *5/*D. *5 is for upper row, *D is for lower row, so its Hex code is row 2 col 5, or 0x25, whereas Hyphen just below it would be 0x2D. The Octal code is 045, whereas that of Hyphen would be 055. In C a preceding 0 (Zero) indicates Octal Constant.

To find the Decimal code of %, note the row label (32-39) and count along to give 37.

Appendix C

ANSI Standard Library Functions

This Appendix provides a quick reference to those library functions recommended by the ANSI Standard. It is divided into three sections:

1. Families of Functions
Functions are first grouped by the header File in which they are declared, e.g. `<stdio.h>`.

2. List of Variables denoting Argument Types
A list of the Variables employed as Arguments or assigned returned Values in section 3. The name of the Variable characterises the Argument Type.

3. Alphabetical list of Functions
A brief description of each Function is given, together with a sample calling Statement. Instead of the C convention of documenting Argument Types by exhibiting a so-called "function prototype", the calling Statement employs a choice of Variable from section 2 having a Name which denotes its Type. This permits an Argument definition which is much closer to how a call would actually appear in a Program. Each entry in the list has the form:

```
Function_Name <library>: sample calling
Statement; ...brief description...
```

1. Families of Functions

Input and Output `<stdio.h>`

```
fopen freopen fflush fclose remove rename tmpfile
setvbuf setbuf
fprintf printf sprintf vprintf vsprintf
```

```
fscanf scanf sscanf
fgetc fgets fputc fputs getc getchar gets putc
putchar puts ungetc
fread fwrite fseek ftell rewind fgetpos fsetpos
clearerr feof ferror perror
```

Character Class Tests <ctype.h>

```
isalnum isalpha iscntrl isdigit isgraph islower
isprint ispunct isspace isupper isxdigit
```

String Functions <string.h>

```
strcpy strncpy strcat strncat strcmp strncmp
strchr strrchr strspn strcspn strpbrk strstr
strlen strerror strtok
memcpy memmove memcmp memchr memset
```

Mathematical Functions <math,h>

```
sin cos tan asin acos atan atan2 sinh cosh tanh exp
log log10 pow sqrt ceil floor fabs ldexp frexp modf
fmod
```

Utility Functions <stdlib.h>

```
atof atoi atol strtod strtol strtoul rand srand
calloc malloc realloc free abort exit atexit
system getenv bsearch qsort abs labs div ldiv
```

Diagnostics <assert.h>

```
assert
```

Variable Argument Lists <stdarg.h>

```
va_start va_arg va_end
```

Non-local Jumps <setjmp.h>

```
setjmp longjmp
```

Signals <signal.h>

```
signal raise
```

Date and Time Functions `<time.h>`

`clock time difftime mktime asctime ctime strftime`

2. Variables denoting Argument Types

The following are employed in section 3 to represent Arguments and Returned Values having each given Type which occurs:

Logical Expression: `(a>5)`

Pointer to Function: `myfun, compare`

`(va_list) ap` (argument pointer defined in `<stdarg.h>`)

`(int) b` (to hold a Truth Value)

`(char) c, ch`

`(double) d, d1, d2, e`

`(double *) dp`

`(float) f, g`

`(FILE *) fp`

`(fpos_t) sav`

`(int) i, j, k, n`

`(unsigned int) ui`

`(int *) ip`

`(long) l, m`

`(int) ok` (to hold a Truth Value indicating succeed/fail)

`(void *) p, q, r` (Pointers to arbitrary objects)

`(char *) name, name2, s, s1, s2, t` (string pointers)

`(char) str[LEN]` (String with Memory assigned to it)

`(char **) endp`

`(jmp_buf) env` (used by `<longjmp.h>`)

`(size_t) size, nobj, n1`

`(time_t) ti, time1, time2`

`(time_t *) tp`

`(struct tm *) ts`

`(div_t) qr` (Structure of `(int) quot, rem`)

`(ldiv_t) lqr` (Structure of `(long) quot, rem`)

3. Alphabetical List of Functions

`abort <stdlib.h>`: `abort();` terminates Program abnormally.

`abs <stdlib.h>`: `j = abs(i);` absolute value of `(int) i`.

`acos <math.h>`: `e = acos(d);` arc cosine of d.

`asctime <time.h>`: `s = asctime(ts);` converts (structure) time into string.

`asin <math.h>`: `e = asin(d);` arc sine of d.

assert <assert.h>: assert(a>5); aborts with diagnostic error message if (a>5) not True.

atan <math.h>: e = atan(d); arc tangent of d.

atan2 <math.h>: e = atan2(d1,d2); arc tangent of d1/d2 in range -π to +π.

atexit <stdlib.h>: atexit(myfun); specifies myfun to be run upon normal termination.

atof <stdlib.h>: d = atof(s); converts s to (double).

atoi <stdlib.h>: i = atoi(s); converts s to (int).

atol <stdlib.h>: l = atol(s); converts s to (long).

bsearch <stdlib.h>: p = bsearch(q, r, n1, size, compare); performs table lookup of q in table specified by r, n1, size.

calloc <stdlib.h>: p = calloc(nobj, size); gets Memory of nobj objects of size (in Bytes).

ceil <math.h>: e = ceil(d); d rounded up to nearest whole number.

clearerr <stdio.h>: clearerr(fp); clears end-of-file and error flags of file: *fp.

clock <time.h>: ti = clock(); returns processor time since start of execution.

cos <math.h>: e = cos(d); cosine of d.

cosh <math.h>: e = cosh(d); hyperbolic cosine of d.

ctime <time.h>: s = ctime(tp); converts calendar time into local time (string).

difftime <time.h>: d = difftime(time2, time1); returns interval in seconds.

div <stdlib.h>: qr = div(i, j); returns (int) {quotient, remainder} of i/j.

exit <stdlib.h>: exit(i); terminates Program normally with status i.

exp <math.h>: e = exp(d); exp(1) to the power of d.

fabs <math.h>: e = fabs(d); absolute value of d.

fclose <stdio.h>: ok = fclose(fp); closes file *fp.

feof <stdio.h>: b = feof(fp); indicates if end-of-file reached for file: *fp.

ferror <stdio.h>: b = ferror(fp); indicates if error has occurred for file: *fp.

fflush <stdio.h>: ok = fflush(fp); writes out buffered data.

fgetc <stdio.h>: ch = fgetc(fp); inputs next Character from file: *fp.

`fgetpos` <stdio.h>: ok = fgetpos(fp, sav); saves current file position, for use by `fsetpos()`.

`fgets` <stdio.h>: s = fgets(s1, n, fp); inputs next String up to Newline from file: *fp.

`floor` <math.h>: e = floor(d); d rounded down to nearest whole number.

`fmod` <math.h>: e = fmod(d1, d2); remainder of d1/d2.

`fopen` <stdio.h>: fp = fopen(name, t); opens the file: name according to mode: t.

`fprintf` <stdio.h>: n = fprintf(fp, t, ...); writes Values: ..., to file: *fp according to format: t.

`fputc` <stdio.h>: c = fputc(ch, fp); outputs Character ch to file: *fp, returns char just written, else EOF.

`fputs` <stdio.h>: i = fputs(s, fp); outputs String: s to file: *fp. Returns (i>0) if ok, else EOF.

`fread` <stdio.h>: n1 = fread(p, size, nobj, fp); inputs from file: *fp (n1<=nobj) arbitrary objects into *p.

`free` <stdlib.h>: free(p); releases Memory starting at *p.

`freopen` <stdio.h>: fp = freopen(name, t); opens the file: name according to mode: t, closing file: name if already opened.

`frexp` <math.h>: d2 = frexp(d, ip); splits d into exponent(power of 2) and mantissa (.5<d2<1).

`fscanf` <stdio.h>: n = fscanf(fp, t, ...); reads from file: *fp into Variables: ..., according to format: t.

`fseek` <stdio.h>: ok = fseek(fp, l, i); alters the position of the File Pointer.

`fsetpos` <stdio.h>: ok = fsetpos(fp, sav); restores current file position as set by `fsetpos()`.

`ftell` <stdio.h>: l = ftell(fp); returns the position of the File Pointer.

`fwrite` <stdio.h>: n1 = fwrite(p, size, nobj, fp); outputs to file: *fp (n1<=nobj) arbitrary objects starting at *p.

`getc` <stdio.h>: ch = getc(fp); inputs next Character from file: *fp (c/f fgetc(), but may be a Macro).

`getchar` <stdio.h>: ch = getchar(); equivalent to: ch = getc(stdin);

`getenv` <stdlib.h>: s = getenv(name); gets String Value of DOS environment Variable: name.

`gets` <stdio.h>: s = gets(s1); inputs next line from keyboard into string s1 (and s).

`gmtime <time.h>:` ts = gmtime(tp); converts calendar time into UTC time.

`isalnum <ctype.h>:` b = isalnum(c); c is a...z A...Z 0 1...9.

`isalpha <ctype.h>:` b = isalpha(c); c is a...z A...Z.

`iscntrl <ctype.h>:` b = iscntrl(c); c is a control character.

`isdigit <ctype.h>:` b = isdigit(c); c is 0 1...9.

`isgraph <ctype.h>:` b = isgraph(c); c is a graphic Character.

`islower <ctype.h>:` b = islower(c); c is a...z.

`isprint <ctype.h>:` b = isprint(c); c is a printing Character including Space.

`ispunct <ctype.h>:` b = ispunct(c); c is a printing Character but not a...z A...Z 0 1...9.

`isspace <ctype.h>:` b = isspace(c); c is Space, Newline Formfeed, Carriage Return, Tab, Vert Tab.

`isupper <ctype.h>:` b = isupper(c); c is A...Z.

`isxdigit <ctype.h>:` b = isxdigit(c); c is a valid hex digit.

`labs <stdlib.h>:` m = labs(l); absolute value of (long) l.

`ldexp <math.h>:` e = ldexp(d, n); d doubled n times.

`ldiv <stdlib.h>:` lqr = ldiv(l, m); returns (long) {quotient, remainder} of l/m.

`localtime <time.h>:` ts = localtime(tp); converts calendar time into local time (structure).

`log <math.h>:` e = log(d); natural logarithm of d.

`log10 <math.h>:` e = log10(d); logarithm of d to base 10.

`longjmp <setjmp.h>:` longjmp(env, n); performs non-local jump simulating a return from most recent call of setjmp(), but returning val instead of Zero.

`malloc <stdlib.h>:` p = malloc(size); gets Memory of size (in Bytes).

`memchr <string.h>:` r = memchr(p, ch, n); finds first occurrence of ch in first n Bytes of buffer *p.

`memcmp <string.h>:` i = memcmp(p, q, n); c/f strncmp.

`memcpy <string.h>:` r = memcpy(p, q, n); copies n Bytes from buffer *q to buffer *p (not overlapping).

`memmove <string.h>:` r = memmove(p, q, n); c/f memcpy, but can handle overlapping buffers.

`memset <string.h>:` r = memset(p, ch, n); sets first n Bytes of buffer *p to the Value of ch.

`mktime <time.h>:` ti = mktime(ts); converts local time (structure) into calendar time.

`modf <math.h>:` e = modf(d, dp); splits d into whole-number and fractional part (e).

`perror <stdio.h>: perror(s);` prints Value of `errno` in an Error message.

`pow <math.h>: e = pow(d1, d2);` d1 to the power of d2.

`printf <stdio.h>: n = printf(t, ...);` writes Values: ..., to file: `stdout` according to format: t.

`putc <stdio.h>: c = putc(ch, fp);` equivalent to: `c = fputc(ch, fp);`

`putchar <stdio.h>: c = putchar(ch);` equivalent to: `c = putc(ch, stdout);`

`puts <stdio.h>: ok = puts(s);` writes String: s, followed by Newline, to `stdout`.

`qsort <stdlib.h>: qsort(r, n1, size, compare);` quick-sorts table specified by `r, n1, size`.

`raise <signal.h>: b = raise(i);` sends signal-type: i to the Program. If successful then b is False (b==0). See `signal()`.

`rand <stdlib.h>: i = rand();` random integer in range 0..32767.

`realloc <stdlib.h>: q = realloc(p, size);` gets (more) Memory of `size` (in Bytes) starting at `*p`.

`remove <stdio.h>: ok = remove(name);` erases file: name.

`rename <stdio.h>: ok = rename(name, name2);` renames file: name to: name2.

`rewind <stdio.h>: rewind(fp);` resets the File Pointer to the start of the File.

`scanf <stdio.h>: n = scanf(t, ...);` reads from file: `stdin` into Variables: ..., according to format: t.

`setbuf <stdio.h>: setbuf(fp, s);` requests default buffering.

`setjmp <setjmp.h>: i = setjmp(env);` marks a target (Statement) for `longjmp()`, saving the environment in (`jmp_buf`) env.

`setvbuf <stdio.h>: ok = setvbuf(fp, s, t, size);` requests special buffering for file: `*fp`.

`signal <signal.h>: p = signal(i, myfun);` temporarily applies handling function: `*myfun` to signal of type: i.

`sin <math.h>: e = sin(d);` sine of d.

`sinh <math.h>: e = sinh(d);` hyperbolic sine of d.

`sprintf <stdio.h>: n = sprintf(s, t, ...);` writes Values: ..., to string: s according to format: t.

`sqrt <math.h>: e = sqrt(d);` square root of d.

`srand <stdlib.h>: srand(ui);` initialises random number seed for `rand()`.

`sscanf <stdio.h>: n = sscanf(s t, ...);` reads from string: s into Variables: . . ., according to format: `t`.

`strcat <string.h>`: `s = strcat(s1, s2);` appends `s2` to `s1`.

`strchr <string.h>`: `s = strchr(s1, ch);` finds first occurrence of `ch` in `s1`.

`strcmp <string.h>`: `i = strcmp(s1, s2);` compares `s1`, `s2` lexicographically. `i==0` if equal, `i>0` if `s1>s2`, `i<0` if `s1<s2`.

`strcpy <string.h>`: `s = strcpy(s1, s2);` copies `s2` into `s1`.

`strcspn <string.h>`: `size = strcspn(s1, s2);` length of substring of `s1` of chars NOT within `s2`.

`strerror <string.h>`: `s = strerror(n);` returns error message numbered `n`.

`strftime <time.h>`: `size = strftime(s, n1, t, ts);` formats string: `s` with date/time information c/f `printf()`.

`strlen <string.h>`: `size = strlen(s);` returns number of Bytes in `s` before final Null.

`strncat <string.h>`: `s = strncat(s1, s2, n);` appends at most `n` Bytes of `s2` to `s1`.

`strncmp <string.h>`: `i = strncmp(s1, s2, n);` c/f `strcmp` but matches at most the first `n` Bytes.

`strncpy <string.h>`: `s = strncpy(s1, s2, n);` copies `n` Bytes of `s2` into `s1`.

`strpbrk <string.h>`: `s = strpbrk(s1, s2);` finds first occurrence in `s1` of any char in `s2`.

`strrchr <string.h>`: `s = strrchr(s1, ch);` finds last occurrence of `ch` in `s1`.

`strspn <string.h>`: `size = strspn(s1, s2);` length of substring of `s1` of chars within `s2`.

`strstr <string.h>`: `s = strstr(s1, s2);` finds first occurrence in `s1` of `s2`.

`strtod <stdlib.h>`: `d = strtod(s, endp);` converts numeric prefix of `s` to `(double)`.

`strtok <string.h>`: `s = strtok(s1, s2);` searches `s1` for tokens delimited by chars within `s2`.

`strtol <stdlib.h>`: `l = strtol(s, endp, k);` converts numeric prefix of `s` to `(long)` using base `k`.

`strtoul <stdlib.h>`: `ul = strtoul(s, endp, k);` converts numeric prefix of `s` to `(unsigned long)` using base `k`.

`system <stdlib.h>`: `system(s);` sends command `s` to DOS for Execution.

`tan <math.h>`: `e = tan(d);` tangent of `d`.

`tanh <math.h>`: `e = tanh(d);` hyperbolic tangent of `d`.

time <time.h>: ti = time(tp); returns current calendar time.

tmpfile <stdio.h>: fp = tmpfile(); creates a temporary file.

tmpnam <stdio.h>: s = tmpnam(str); generates a unique name for (e.g.) a temporary file.

ungetc <stdio.h>: c = ungetc(ch, fp); pushes back Character: ch onto input file: *fp.

va_arg <stdarg.h>: argn = va_arg(ap, type); gets next Argument in argument line. The symbolic Argument: type identifies to va_arg() the expected Type of argn.

va_end <stdarg.h>: va_end(ap); finishes argument line processing.

va_start <stdarg.h>: va_start(ap, arg); sets-up argument line processing. The symbolic Argument: arg identifies to va_start() the final Argument to be fetched from the argument line.

vfprintf <stdio.h>: vfprintf(fp, t, arg); writes Values: ..., to file: *fp according to format: t.

vprintf <stdio.h>: vprintf(t, arg); writes Values: arg, to file: stdout according to format: t.

vsprintf <stdio.h>: vsprintf(s, t, arg); writes Values: arg, to string: s according to format: t.

Appendix D

The %-Construct of scanf() and printf()

The `<stdio.h>` standard library Functions, `printf()` and `scanf()`, accept a format String which controls the conversion of any Arguments which follow. To each successive Argument there must correspond a suitable "conversion specification" comprising the following Tokens in the given order:

For **scanf()** :

❏ % (the Percent Character). Compulsory.

❏ * (the Asterisk Character). Optional. If present this suppresses any assignment to its Variable as a result of a match.

❏ Maximum input field width (as an unsigned whole number). Optional.

❏ Target Variable width (h, l or L). Only present if the target demands it.

❏ Conversion Character (one of: c d e f g i n o p s u x [..]) Compulsory. See below for their meaning.

❏ An example using all the above: %*35Ld

For **printf()** :

❏ % (the Percent Character). Compulsory.

❏ Flags (one or more of: − + Space 0 #). Optional, in any order. If present the specification is modified as follows:

  ● − (left justification in allocated field)
  ● + (always print the sign, + or −)
  ● Space (pad with single Space if the first printed Character is not + or −)
  ● 0 (numeric conversions only, pad the allocated field with leading zeros)
  ● # (additional output decoration, depending on the conversion Character used)

❏ Minimum output field width (as an unsigned whole number). Optional.

❑ . (Decimal point). Only present if a precision follows.

❑ Precision (as an unsigned whole number). Optional. Means one of the following, depending on the conversion Character used:
- ● no. of Digits after the decimal point (%e %E %f)
- ● no. of significant Digits to be printed (%g %G)
- ● max. no. of Characters from a String (%s)
- ● min. no. of Digits to be printed for an Integer, padded if necessary with leading zeros (%d %i %o %u %x %X)

❑ Target Variable length modifier (h, l or L). Only present if the target demands it.

❑ Conversion Character (one of: c d e E f g G i n o p s u x X) Compulsory. See below for their meaning.

❑ An example using all the above: %-+ 0#10.6Lf

Since "...%..." (Percent) in the format String represents the start of a conversion specification, an isolated % will not be recognised as a literal Percent. Wherever a literal Percent is required, use: %%

The Meaning of the Conversion Characters

In keeping with the book's stress on actual examples, an abstract explanation of each conversion character has been avoided in favour of a single illustrative sample conversion under printf() and sscanf() in turn.

Assume that each of the sample Statements have been preceded by these definitions:

```
int i=255, j=-32768, k=32767, l=0, m=0, n=0;
float f1=1.23456789, f2=(-0.0000000076),
f3=6.023e+23;
char ch='$', s[80], t[80];
void *p;
```

Beneath the printf() Statement is shown what would actually get printed.

Beneath the sscanf() Statement is shown the Values its Arguments would subsequently take.

Using sscanf() instead of scanf() allows the sample input to be shown more succinctly. The behaviour under sscanf() applies also to scanf() and fscanf(). Likewise the behaviour for printf()

applies also to `sprintf()`, `fprintf()`, `vprintf()`, `vfprintf()` and `vsprintf()`.

%c Character
```
printf("LETTER=%c",ch);
   LETTER=$
sscanf("Alpha Bravo","%8c",s);
   s: "Alpha Br"
```

(Contrast this with "`%s`", which would stop matching at the first Space encountered).

%d Decimal
```
printf("%d %d %d",i,j,k);
   255 -32768 32767
sscanf("255 -32768 32767", "%d %d %d",
&l,&m,&n);
   l==255, m==(-32768), n==32767
```

%E Scientific (printf only)
```
printf("%E %E %E",f1,f2,f3);
   1234568E+000 -7.600000E-009 6.023000E+023
```

%e Scientific
```
printf("%e %e %e",f1,f2,f3);
   1234568e+000 -7.600000e-009 6.023000e+023
sscanf("1.23456789 -0.0000000076 6.023e+23",
"%e %e %e",&f1,&f2,&f3);
   f1==1234568e+000, f2==-7.600000e-009,
   f3==6.023000e+023
```

%f Floating-point Decimal
```
printf("%f %f %f",f1,f2,f3);
   1.234568 -0.000000
·602299993035875130000000.00000
sscanf() -- %f same as for %e.
```

%G Decimal or Scientific (printf only)
```
printf("%G %G %G",f1,f2,f3);
   1.234568 -7.6E-009 6.023E+023
```

%g Decimal or Scientific
```
printf("%g %g %g",f1,f2,f3);
   1.234568 -7.6e-009 6.023e+023
sscanf() -- %g same as for %e.
```

%i Integer

```
printf() -- %i same as for %d.
sscanf("037 777 0xff", "%i %i %i",&l,&m,&n);
   l==31, m==777, n==255
```

%n Number of Characters

Takes (int *) argument for both printf and scanf. Writes into it the number of Characters read so far by this call. (Compare the following sample with that for %d above):

```
printf("%d %d%n %d",i,j,&n,k);
   255 -32768 32767
   n==10
sscanf("037 777 0xff", "%i %i%n %i",&i,&j,&n,
&k);
   n==9
```

%o Octal

```
printf("%o %o %o",i,j,k);
   377 100000 77777
sscanf("255 -32768 32767", "%o %o %o",&l,&m,
&n);
   l==173, m==(-1726), n=(unassigned because 8 stopped
   match)
```

%p Pointer

```
p=st; printf("%p %p",p,st);
   005D 005D
sscanf("12ef", "%p", &p); /*NB: arg must be ptr
to a ptr */
   p==0x12ef
```

%s String

```
printf("%s %s","Alpha", "Bravo");
   Alpha Bravo
sscanf("Alpha Bravo","%s %s",s,t);
   s: "Alpha"
   t: "Bravo"
```

%u Unsigned

```
printf("%u %u %u",i,j,k);
   255 32768 32767
sscanf("255 65535 -1", "%u %u %u",
&ui,&uj,&uk);
   ui==, uj==65535, uk==(unassigned)
```

%X Hexadecimal (printf only)
```
printf("%X %4X %04X %X %X",i,i,i,j,k);
   FF FF 00FF 8000 7FFF
```

%x Hexadecimal
```
printf("%X %4X %04X %X %X",i,i,i,j,k);
   ff ff 00ff 8000 7fff
sscanf("037 777 0xff", "%x %x 0x%x",&l,&m,&n);
   l==55, m==1911, n==255
```

%% Literal Percent
```
printf("\nThis is a hundred percent: %d%%.\n",
100);
   This is a hundred percent: 100%.
sscanf("50% 99% ", "%d%% %d%%", &l,&m);
   l==50, m==99
```

%[...] String containing only given Characters (scanf only)
```
sscanf("Alpha Bravo Charlie Delta","%[Apl]
%[abBh ]",s,t);
   s: "Alp"
   t: "ha B"
```

%[^...] String NOT containing given Characters (scanf only)
```
sscanf("Alpha Bravo Charlie Delta","%[^ ]
%[^DE]",s,t);
   s: "Alpha"
   t: "Bravo Charlie "
```